"These are sorrowful voices, and the waste is everywhere: waste of beauty,
talent, grace. Sometimes their powerful exuberance rises up and you
believe they have a shot at happiness." —*Los Angeles Times*

"*I Am an Emotional Creature* is thoughtful and provocative. Its unbiased
acceptance of girls of all types is comforting and inspiring."
—The Associated Press

"A searing look at the inner lives of young females today in entries that
explore sex, violence, love, body image, materialism, identity, family,
friends, and the future [and] a potent call to girls to honor their emotions
and to readers of all ages to uphold human rights at every level, from the
boardroom to the bedroom." —*Booklist*

"Leave it to Eve Ensler to get it right. Her new book, *I Am an Emotional
Creature,* made me want to vomit from its emotional power. Ensler does
not coddle the reader; instead she forces us to realize that teenage girls
possess the largest untapped energy source in the world. . . . Ultimately all
about girls, this is a tale about dreams, nightmares, realities, boyfriends,
fathers, body image, sports, friendship, popularity, mothers, piercings,
and poetry. It's the God's honest truth, as my mother would say." —*Bust*

"In all the years I've been working with adolescent girls and their moms, I
have not found a single book that I could recommend to both, until now.
Eve Ensler's latest masterpiece is so powerful that every mom and her
teen daughter should have her own personal copy. . . . It is a call to action
for every girl to find, use and celebrate her authentic voice." —Tonic.com

"Insightful." —*Teen Vogue*

"The collection shines when dealing with more serious material. . . . The
average American teenager should gain a good bit of perspective."
—*Publishers Weekly*

"If you know a young lady, young man, parents of a daughter . . . or pretty
much anyone who is or comes in contact with a female, recommend this
book." —*Roanoke Times*

I AM
AN EMOTIONAL
CREATURE

I AM
AN EMOTIONAL
CREATURE

THE SECRET LIFE OF GIRLS AROUND THE WORLD

Eve Ensler

VILLARD TRADE PAPERBACKS

NEW YORK

2011 Villard Books Trade Paperback Edition

Published in the United States by Villard, an imprint of The Random
House Publishing Group, a division of Random House, Inc., New York.

VILLARD BOOKS and VILLARD & "V" CIRCLED Design are
registered trademarks of Random House, Inc.

Originally published in hardcover in the United States by Villard Books,
an imprint of The Random House Publishing Group, a division
of Random House, Inc., in 2010.

Library of Congress Cataloging-in-Publication Data
Ensler, Eve.
I am an emotional creature: the secret life of girls
around the world / Eve Ensler.
p.   cm.
Includes bibliographical references.
ISBN 978-0-8129-7016-6
1. Girls—Psychology.   2. Girls—Social conditions—21st century.
3. Girls—Social life and customs—21st century.   I. Title.
HQ777.E57 2010
155.43'3—dc22   2009044775

Printed in the United States of America

www.villard.com

468975

Book design by Caroline Cunningham

For Colette and Charlotte

GIRL FACT

Your left lung is smaller than your right lung

to make room for your heart.

AUTHOR'S NOTE

These monologues are not interviews. Each monologue is a lit-
erary text inspired by traveling the world, by witnessing events,
by listening to real and imagined conversations. On occasion a
monologue was inspired by an article, an experience, a memory,
a dream, a wish, an image, or a moment of grief or rage.

FOREWORD

Carol Gilligan

Having broken a rather astonishing silence by encouraging
women to say "vagina" in public, Eve Ensler has now written a
new set of monologues, intended this time for girls. "Dear Emotional Creature," she begins in an introduction that is at once a
cri de coeur and a call to action. As a woman, she knows the
pressures on girls to silence themselves, to act as if they have no
feelings or their feelings do not matter, to please everyone except themselves. The simple statement "I am an emotional creature" becomes a challenge to the myriad ways in which girls are
looked at but not seen, talked about but not listened to, used,
discarded, violated, exploited, maimed, and even killed. Like a
woman claiming her body, a girl claiming her emotions breaks a
silence and unleashes a vast resource of clean energy, an energy
that can inspire all of us to transform and heal the world.

In addition to the girl facts recorded in this book, there is another series of facts worth considering: throughout the years of childhood, girls are more psychologically robust and resilient than boys, less depressed, less likely to suffer from learning and speech disorders, less likely to harm themselves and other people. The initiation of young boys into a masculinity that requires them to cover their emotional natures, to sacrifice love for the sake of honor and wed themselves to a false story about themselves, has its parallel in the initiation of girls at adolescence into the division between good and bad women, the worshipped and the despised. As an honest voice comes to sound or seem stupid or crazy, as girls are pressed to internalize a misogyny built into the very structure of patriarchy, in which being a man means not being a woman and also being on top, a resistance wells up inside them, grounded in their human nature. Like the healthy body, the healthy psyche resists disease, and girls being adolescents at the time of their initiation are for this reason more lie-resistant. Hence the power of girls' voices to expose, and by exposing disrupt what otherwise goes on for the most part in silence.

I remember the day I went to the Boston Museum of Fine Arts with a group of eleven- and twelve-year-old girls. We were spending a week together, doing writing and theater exercises as part of a project designed to strengthen girls' healthy resistance and courage. In the coatroom of the museum, as the girls shed backpacks and raincoats, I said we were going to be investigative reporters: our assignment was to discover how women appear in this museum. "Naked," Emma said, without hesitation. A current of recognition ran silently, swiftly, through the group. Later, when asked to write a conversation with one of the women in the museum, Emma chose a headless, armless Greek statue, weaving into the conventions of polite conversation her two burning questions: "Are you cold?" and "Do you want some clothes?" The statue's response, "I have no money," leads Emma to say that she knows a place where they give away clothes: "It's right around the corner." At which point, Emma and the statue leave the museum.

The monologues in this book are scripts for girls' resistance. Traveling around the world on behalf of V-Day, the movement Eve founded to end violence against women and girls, she was drawn repeatedly to the teenage girls she met along the way. Captivated by an electric energy that was in danger of being hijacked, she turned her writer's eye and ear to conserving this energy by transforming it into pieces for girls to perform. Wise, funny, irreverent, shocking, the monologues give voice to what girls know. We hear a girl's pleasure in wearing a short skirt and feeling the wind against her legs, her fear of being fat or hungry, her terror in finding herself sold into sex slavery, her desire to escape from those who in one way or another, whether with the best or worst of intentions, would deny or override her emotional nature.

The ten years I spent listening to girls, charting their development, going with them to beaches and museums, writing and doing theater work with them, had the cast of revelation. Passages from my journal recording pleasures unearthed and losses covered over bring back the visceral sensations of that time:

This morning in the shower, I remember what it was like on Monday, that intense experience of pleasure, seeing the girls

at the beach—their bodies, their freedom. Minnow-like
bodies darting in and out of the water. Running on the sand.
Dancing, turning. I began to remember an eleven-year-old
body—I began to remember my eleven-year-old body and to
enter that body. Without thinking I began running, unen-
cumbered, fast like the wind.

. . .

Covering loss with words. Embroidering beauty over the
ragged hole of loss. An inner sadness and a sign: Do not
touch. I am touched so directly, so immediately by these
girls. . . . I begin to move directly in their presence, to
speak without hesitation, to find a freedom and pleasure
that I relish. . . . To leave this is to face the sadness of its
loss. . . .

The research with girls was taking me back into what had
been a lost time, a moment of freedom before womanhood set in.
The sound of girls' voices, at once familiar and surprising,
brought home the extent to which I and other women have
rewritten our histories to conform to a story I now recognized as
untrue. Like Anne Frank rewriting her diary, I had muted my
pleasure with my mother. Like thirteen-year-old Tracy, I had
come to hear an honest voice as "stupid." Like sixteen-year-old
Iris, I feared that "if I were to say what I was feeling and thinking,
no one would want to be with me, my voice would be too loud."
Like Iris, I knew that "you have to have relationships," while at
the same time I knew that relationships maintained by silencing
myself were not relationships in any meaningful sense.

I Am an Emotional Creature was written for girls. As Eve says, it is "a call to question rather than to please." It is also a call to all of us to join girls' resistance to turning their backs on one another and themselves. The opposite of patriarchy is democracy, rooted in voice rather than in violence and honed through relationship. Whether read in silence or performed on a stage, these monologues carry the hope of recalling us to our better selves. They remind us of a store of energy in our midst that doesn't cost anything and does not pollute, a source of power waiting to be set free. To understand the forces marshaled against its release is to recognize the extent to which we are held captive to a false story about ourselves, a story about manhood and womanhood that belies the fact that, as humans, we are all emotional creatures.

CONTENTS

INTRODUCTION

Dear Emotional Creature,

You know who you are. I wrote this book because I believe in
you. I believe in your authenticity, your uniqueness, your inten-
sity, your wildness. I love the way you dye your hair purple, or
hike up your short skirt, or blare your music while you lip-sync
every single memorized lyric. I love your restlessness and your
hunger. You are one of our greatest natural resources. You possess a necessary agency and energy that if unleashed could
transform, inspire, and heal the world.

I know we make you feel stupid, as if being a teenager
meant you were temporarily deranged. We have become accus-
tomed to muting you, judging you, discounting you, asking you—
sometimes even forcing you—to betray what you see and know
and feel.

You scare us. You remind us of what we have been forced to
shut down or abandon in ourselves in order to fit in. You ask us
by your being to question, to wake up, to reperceive. Sometimes

I think we tell you we are protecting you when really we are protecting ourselves from our own feelings of self-betrayal and loss.

Everyone seems to have a certain way they want you to be—your mother, father, teachers, religious leaders, politicians, boyfriends, fashion gurus, celebrities, girlfriends. In researching this book I came upon a very disturbing statistic: 74 percent of you say you are under pressure to please everyone.

I have done a lot of thinking about what it means to please. To please, to embody the wish or will of somebody other than yourself. To please the fashion setters, we starve ourselves. To please boys, we push ourselves when we aren't ready. To please the popular girls, we end up acting mean to our best friends. To please our parents, we become insane overachievers. If you are trying to please, how do you take responsibility for your own needs? How do you even know what your own needs are? What do you have to cut off in yourself in order to please others? I think the act of pleasing makes everything murky. We lose track of ourselves. We stop uttering declaratory sentences. We stop directing our lives. We wait to be rescued. We forget what we know. We make everything okay rather than real.

I have had the good fortune to travel around the world. Everywhere I meet teenage girls, circles of girls, packs of girls walking the country roads home from school, hanging out on city street corners, arm in arm, laughing, giggling, screaming. Electric girls. I see how your lives get hijacked, how your opinions and desires get denied and undone. I see too how this later comes to determine so much of our lives as adults. So many of the women I have met through *The Vagina Monologues* and *The Good Body* and V-Day are still trying to overcome what was muted or undone in them when they were young. They are struggling late into their lives to know their desires, to find their power and their way.

This book is a call to question rather than to please. To provoke, to challenge, to dare, to satisfy your own imagination and appetite. To know yourself truly. To take responsibility for who you are, to engage. This book is a call to listen to the voice inside you that might want something different, that hears, that knows, the way only you can hear and know. It's a call to your original girl self, to your emotional creature self, to move at your speed, to walk with your step, to wear your color. It is an invitation to heed your instinct to resist war, or draw snakes, or to speak to the stars.

I hope you will see this book as something living, that you will use it to help you to identify and overcome the obstacles or pressures that prevent you from being an emotional creature. Maybe after you read these stories and monologues you will be inspired to write and share your own, or paint your bedroom wall or fight for polar bears or speak up in class or learn about sexuality or demand your rights.

When I was your age, I didn't know how to live as an emotional creature. I felt like an alien. I still do a lot of the time. I don't think it has much to do with the country I grew up in or the language I speak. In this book you will meet girls from everywhere. Some live in remote villages, others in huge cities or posh suburbs. Some worrying about whether they will be able to afford the latest purple UGGs, some worrying if they'll ever get home after two years of being held as a sex slave. Some deciding whether they are able to kill a supposed enemy, some on the brink of killing themselves, some desperate for the next meal, some unable to stop starving themselves. Girls from Cairo, Kwai Yong, Sofia, Ramallah, Bukavu, Narok, Westchester, Jerusalem, Manhattan, Paris. All of them, all of you, live on the planet right now. I think whatever country or town or village you physically live in, you inhabit a similar emotional landscape. You all come from girl land. There you get born with this awakeness, this open-hearted have to eat it, taste it, know it, defy it. Then the "grown-ups" come with their rules, their directions. They teach you how to make yourselves less so everyone feels more comfortable. They teach you not to stand out. They get you to behave.

I am older now. I finally know the difference between pleasing and loving, obeying and respecting. It has taken me so many years to be okay with being different, with being this alive, this intense. I just don't want you to have to wait that long.

Love,
Eve

Section I

YOU TELL ME HOW TO BE A GIRL IN 2010

Questions, doubt, ambiguity, and dissent
have somehow become very unmasculine.
Authoritarian maniacs are
premiers, czars, and presidents.
Each one is more righteous than the next.
Each town they bomb
each human they kill
is done for "humanitarian" purposes.

People don't own the water in their own village
and they certainly don't own the diamonds and gold.
Millions are forced to make dinner out of garbage and dust
while Russian businessmen and movie stars
are buying 500-million-euro villas on Côte Sud.

Bees have stopped making honey.
People are drilling in all the wrong places.

The U.S., Russia, Canada, Denmark, and Norway all claim the
    Arctic
but none of them seem to care that the polar bears are drowning.

They are fingerprinting, photographing our licenses and teeth.
Big Brother is now in our phones, our pods, our PCs.
Not one of us feels even a little safer.
New Age mental health providers turn
out to be former war torturers with beards.
And the pope in a dress showing off his
ermine trim and cuffs
is telling everyone that
people kissing people they love is the greatest evil.
A woman running for U.S. vice president
believes in creationism
but not global warming.

Why is everyone so much more afraid of sex
than SCUD missiles?
And who decided God wasn't into pleasure?
And if the hetero nuclear family is so great
how come everyone is fleeing it
or paying their life savings just
to sit in a room with a stranger and cry about it?

The Iraq war cost nearly $3 trillion.
I can't even count that high
but I know
that money could have

would have
ended poverty in general
which would have canceled terrorism.
How come we have money to kill
but no money to feed or heal?
How come we have money to destroy
but no money for art and schools?

The fundamentalists now have
billion-dollar private armies.
The Taliban is back
but never went away.
Women are burned, raped, bludgeoned, sold,
starved, and buried alive
and still don't know they are the majority.

Water is clearly nearly running out
but even in the desert where there's serious drought
the golf courses are green and lush
and the swimming pools are full of water
for the twelve rich people who might decide to come.

Special people adopt hand-picked babies in faraway lands.
Their flights there cost more
than the babies' parents made
this year.
Why don't they just give it to them?
Slavery is back
but never went away.

Just ask anyone who's been whipped
how deep the legacy.
Six million dead in the Congo
and they never made the news,
and don't tell me it doesn't have
to do with color
and minerals.

Poor folks are dying first
From hurricanes
Shame
Tsunamis
Radiation
Pollution
Floods
And neglect.
Rich folks
just put up fancier super-electrified gates
on their private perfect cities.

Everyone's having "benefits"
and throwing fancy parties
with lots of swag
so the rich people feel good about giving
away the tiny little bit of the whole lot they have.
But no one really wants to change anything.
If you really want it
you have to give something up
like everything

and then those that have, wouldn't,
and then who would they be?
And that's too complicated
so they write checks
and keep doing the same old things.
Selling change.
Making revolution profitable.
Corporations own everything anyway
even our hippie jeans, memory cells, and rain.
Why do so many women leaders look like Margaret Thatcher
and act even meaner?
Why doesn't anyone remember anything?
And how come rich bad people
get paid lots of money to give speeches
and poor bad people are tortured
and in prisons?
Is there anyone in charge?
Or is this whole thing spinning out until it explodes
or dissolves?
And if there is something we can do
why aren't we doing it?
What happened to fury?
What happened to accuracy
or accountability?
What happened to not showing off your wealth?
What happened to kindness?
What happened to teenagers rebelling
instead of buying and selling?
What happened to teenagers kissing

instead of blogging and dissing?
What happened to teenagers marching
and refusing
instead of exploiting and using?

I want to touch you in real time
not find you on YouTube,
I want to walk next to you in the mountains
not friend you on Facebook.
Give me one thing I can believe in
that isn't a brand name.

I'm lonely.
I'm scared.
Girls younger than me are giving blowjobs
in homeroom
and they don't even know it's sex.
They just want to be popular
and get some respect.
Most girls my age are taking pills
or not getting out of bed
or eating or starving
or getting nose jobs or implants
or getting cut
or twittering away
or covering themselves
or desperate for a way
to be awake without faking
to be alive without freaking

to be serious
to be true
to even think of loving someone
when we're already doomed.

You tell me how to be a girl in 2010

I say let's go for it
if it's all coming down.
I say let's speak it
let's fight it
let's right it
there's nothing to hold on to
if it's already gone.
They left it to us.
It sucks but it's true.
It's you and me baby.

LET ME IN

Suburbs, USA

Oh God. I hate it when they act like that.

"Sit down. Shut up. Stop embarrassing me. Please!"

Don't worry!

I don't say this out loud. God no. Only in my head. These are my friends . . . supposedly.

"Oh God. Please stop. You are so utterly immature."

I hate it when all those people look at me.

Not like them. They're always showing off. They're not so sure of themselves when they're alone. But in the posse—giddyup.

It's hopeless. I can't keep up. I'm always one Marc Jacobs, one Juicy Couture behind.

There's Julie.

"Hi hi." Kiss kiss.

She hates my guts. Look at her cruising my once-something-now-so-over boot. I wish my feet were leaves. Blow away. I bought the brown leather riding boots like you said. Even though I'm allergic to horses and I didn't have the money. Or I should say my mother didn't. She's a temp secretary and sometimes for weeks doesn't even get called. I got hysterical in the shoe store. Started hyperventilating on the floor. My mother was so embarrassed that she paid.

But then they changed right after that. Julie says riding boots are so pre-Britney. It's all about purple UGGs. My mother will not even consider it. She doesn't get it. She constantly jeopardizes my position. I mean she's the reason I can't keep up. I hate my mother and I hate these painful riding boots even more. To be honest I didn't like them in the first place. Now I just look like a stupid girl without a pony.

Oh God, Julie just can't stop.

"Cut it out, okay? I got the drop circle earrings like you said and the . . . Just stop checking me out."

Don't worry. I don't say this out loud. Only in my head. They are my friends . . . supposedly.

Julie now hates every bit of me. It happened yesterday. I completely blew it. I was accidentally nice to Wendy Apple in front of them. I forgot and hugged her right there. I lost myself. Wendy is so out. She's got wild hair and her family lives in this ugly house and she has the dumbest laugh. She can't help herself and she really doesn't care. To be honest, I sort of like Wendy. Well, I admire her. She's pretty sarcastic and draws these amazing pictures of slutty angels who are always falling from somewhere like outer space. But it's familiar.

Julie says she's not like us. Well, *them*. Julie saw me hug Wendy and did the big eyeball roll in front of all of the posse like I was demented or pathetic and then she turned her back on me. So did they. Like her backup dancers.

So I got mad at Wendy. I shoved her a little and turned my head and told Wendy to stay away from me. She just looked at me, stared in shock like I was an alien. Then she started crying. That made me feel pretty shitty because I kind of like her a lot. But it made Julie like me again. Later Julie gave me the same kind of glitter lipstick that Beyoncé wore at the MTV music awards. Julie only used it for two weeks.

But she is suspicious. So are the others. The word is out. It's because of my clunky boots and my tits. Well, my lack of them. Julie is stacked and that's why all the greatest guys are after her. She and Bree rule the posse. They don't go anywhere apart. Even to pee. I saw them go into the toilet together. They were laughing real loud and we were all wondering if it was us they were laughing at. Wendy told me they had padded bras and went all the way. That's why the guys like them so much. But Julie is genuinely pretty and very skinny. Her stomach is totally wholly abbed and flat like Gwen Stefani's and she's got that "I can't help it if I'm perfect" smile. Bree's hair is actually a little frizzy but she's got perfect breasts and the coolest voice all deep like Miley and she doesn't even have to fake it. She was born like that. Bree brought me into the posse 'cause I helped her with her history exam. She definitely regrets it now. I am the contaminator. Loser-girl virus. It spreads so fast, and once you get it you're forever dead and ugly.

Oh God. Look at them. They can't even go to the vending machine without each other. Aren't they happy?

I shouldn't be telling you this. Breaking confidentiality. Totally illegal. We signed this posse agreement, really cool like Angelina Jolie's personal assistants do.

But sometimes I want to say:

"Grow up. Be real. Stop pretending. Leave me alone."

Don't worry, I don't say this out loud. Only in my head. These are my friends . . . supposedly.

But the reason they hate Wendy Apple so much is 'cause she was one of them once. Higher up than Bree. I mean, she could have been a Julie. What Wendy did was like a revolutionary. She just gave it up. I mean, she walked away. She said it was stupid. And she told everyone their secrets. Even the ugliest and fattest girls know about their padded bras. Julie and Bree tried to sue. But the posse agreement didn't really hold up in high school court.

I can't believe it. Julie and Bree are all over Amber. That's because of Amber's older brother who Julie is suddenly dating. Amber made this happen, and so now Julie is just worshipping her. I mean, God, you would think Amber would be embarrassed. Two weeks ago Julie and Bree humiliated her in the locker room, did the posse circle in the shower when Amber was naked and we all laughed at her body.

You know Wendy wrote me a note in third period and said she wasn't crying for herself. She said she was crying for me 'cause I started out so nice and now I am so desperate. But I'm not funny like Wendy or talented. I am so tragically in the middle. Not one outstanding characteristic. I have nothing going for me . . . but them.

Wait a minute. There's no more room at the table. Tiffany was supposed to get there first and save me a seat. But Tiffany is sitting in between Julie and Bree.

Oh God, look at my boots—they are so stupid. And my hair, I hate it. My mother can't even get work as a typist. I'm just a pathetic blob of middle girl.

"Please don't do this. Make room at the table. Tiffany, what about my seat? Don't squeeze me out. Tiffany, stop pretending I'm not here. Oh look, look. Julie is braiding your hair. So now you're Julie's friend. Tiffany! Tiffany, turn around! I am here. I am not dead. What? What?"

Bree is motioning them to cut me off. They're giving me the posse slam.

"Don't do that. Bree, remember I helped you pass the exam? I gave you the answers and risked my ass. Listen. I don't like these riding boots. I bought them for you. I know you were really generous to let me in because I am so utterly insignificant. I know I don't have breasts. I'll get the UGGs. I promise. I won't be nice to people you hate. I'll do whatever you want. Please. Please just let me sit down. Make room on the bench. Let me in. Let me in. Let me in!!"

Oh God. Everyone is looking. I must be really screaming. It's in the cafeteria and not just in my head.

(*Tantrum*)

"I can't do it, Julie. I can't keep up. I will never be invited. I won't ever get the guy. My hair is stringy and ugly and my breasts don't exist. I am a piece of shit shit shit. Let me in. Let me in."

(*She collapses.*)

(*She wakes up.*)

I wake up at Wendy's. There is incense burning that smells like fruit. Apples, I think. Right. Wendy Apple. I don't remember how I got here. Wendy is sitting next to the bed, drawing a picture of me as an angel in transition. She says I have hit bottom. And that it feels terrible now. But I am lucky it has happened so young. She says she will be my friend if I can stop worrying about being popular. She says there are others who don't fit in and I will like them better. She says there is another world and the door is open. She says she can help.

Wendy laughs and it's too loud. I want to be pretty. Wendy is incredibly kind. I want to be skinny. Wendy is on the outside. And I am no one. Wendy is by my bed and she is drawing my picture.

WHAT DON'T YOU LIKE ABOUT BEING A GIRL?

Girls can't control anything
Boys can do anything they want
My brother is adored,
I am ignored
My boobs, people talking about my boobs
People assuming you can't do something
My boobs, it all changed with my boobs
Blood, cramps, seven days
People thinking you are weak
A girl can get pregnant
You have to do your hair
You have to remove your hair
Wash and iron clothes
More chance of being raped
Have to take care of husbands and kids
Girls can't work even though
they are educated.

GIRL FACT

One in five U.S. high school girls say they do not
know three adults to turn to if
they have a problem.

BAD BOYS

New York, New York

I like bad boys
It's the danger
He goes to boarding school
He's a darker person
Sort of like me
We're both troubled
I'm better at hiding it
I cut myself
Trying to find something I'm good at
My father is very successful
High expectations
I fail them a lot
I'm not the person they want me to be
My mother wants a perfect family
I don't believe in perfection
Perfect in my mother's world:
Straight A's

Super-thin
Being intelligent and happy
Really good at everything
I don't know who I am
Cutting myself
Trying to control
Everything crashing down on me
It became a release

I gave my mother a poem
She sent me to a shrink
My shrink
gave me a rubber band
to put on my wrist
Rather than cutting I snap myself

Mom wants me to be a model
She weighs me every day
She weighs herself twice a day
I started to make myself throw up just
so my mother would leave me alone.
My best friend shoots Ritalin to lose weight
Everyone pretends they have ADD
You get extra time on the tests
and you do better which will
get you into an Ivy League college
I feel absolutely alone in the world
The things my mother would like to change about me:
I'm disorganized

I wear big boots in summer
Have grungy vintage clothing
I listen to weird loud music
I feel a connection with Sylvia Plath
I cut my own hair
Hacked my bangs into pieces
She flipped out
She wants me in Ralph Lauren sweaters

My boyfriend went through rough times
He has his own blog
Yesterday he got grounded
He spray-painted a bomb on his bedroom wall
His parents got divorced
He hates his new apartment
He's very angry
Angry at his father for leaving his mother
Angry at the new stupid place where they are living
He is not the most handsome boy
But he's troubled
Like me.

WHAT I WISH I COULD SAY TO MY MOTHER

I don't know you

I'm pregnant

Listen to me

I'm gay and I am not the devil

You can trust me

I know you are unhappy

I don't want to keep taking care of you

Do you like sex?

Do you have it a lot?

Why do you hate your body?

Don't read my journal

Read my journal

Do you think I'm smart?

How come you never tell me?

You're my role model

I wish you liked Dad

I miss Dad

I want you to be happy

GIRL FACTS

Despite years of evaluation in this area, there is no evidence to date that abstinence-only education delays teen sexual activity. Moreover, recent research shows that abstinence-only strategies may deter contraceptive use among sexually active teens, increasing their risk of unintended pregnancy and STIs.

Six in ten American teens have sex before they leave high school, and 730,000 teenage girls will get pregnant this year.

IT'S NOT A BABY, IT'S A MAYBE

(Teenage girl sucking her thumb)
My boyfriend told me to stop sucking my thumb.
He said it was weird and it made me look like a baby.
I never thought about a baby.
It happened fast
and it didn't feel that great.
Well, it almost felt good.
But then he/Carlos stopped
right when it was about to begin for me.
I knew I wasn't supposed to be doing it.
I was practicing abstinence
but to be honest, I didn't really know how to apply it.
'Cause once the kissing starts . . .

I am tired a lot.
My mother thinks I'm doing drugs.
I could never tell her.
She is super-Catholic.

Sometimes I picture it like a new little friend
and we could talk about stuff
and maybe even later she could help me.
But that is really far off
and right now I don't even have a job or an idea
about what I would do.

I wouldn't be attacking it or anything.
I would just be removing it.
I wouldn't hurt it,
just put it someplace else.
It is not a person really.
It's a problem
getting bigger and bigger.

My girlfriend Juicy told me to do the right thing.
Just imagine, she said, if your mama had done that to you.
Well, then I wouldn't have a problem growing inside me
and I wouldn't want to kill myself.

I like school.
I want to be an important person.
I told Juicy, it's not a baby.
It's a maybe.

I dreamed the other night that I took it
out to look at it.
It was really cute and the size of my thumbnail.

It looked like one of those stickers I put on my notebook
with the smiley face.
I tried to put it back in
but this nurse was there.
She looked just like J Lo
except she had really bad hair
like me.
She was all nasty and told me it
was too late
and why'd I take it out 'cause
it was none of my business.
Maybe it means the baby's dead.
That makes me sad
and a little relieved.
I mean I would like to meet her.
I think she might have my face.
I hope she doesn't have my hair and thighs.

I don't really even know Carlos so well.
I mean he's got great clothes
and knows all the rappers—
songs that is.
But he could have craziness in his family
and then this problem would turn into a crazy person
and then I would have to spend my whole life
taking care and worrying that he didn't end up in jail
or paying rent while he was just staring off into space eating Big
Macs all day.

My mother says
if you take a life you go to hell.
But I am already in hell.
I don't even know if I like babies.
I like the baby clothes.
They're all soft and shit, and the little baby shoes
and hats.
I could dress her all nice
but then she would be crying
and not stop crying
and I really wouldn't like that.

WHAT'S A GOOD GIRL?

She doesn't speak to a boy at all

Has morals

Tells the truth even if she pisses people off

Respectable

Doesn't argue

Polite

Quiet

She brings her homework with her

Doesn't step out of the line

Follows her parents in everything

Even if she disagrees

Goes to church every Sunday

Stays in on the weekends

Doesn't know more than she should

Asks questions even if she knows the answers

GIRL FACT

In Africa, about three million girls a year are

at risk for female genital mutilation—

more than 8,000 per day.

DON'T

Cairo, Egypt

Don't look from the window
Don't talk to other girls
Don't go out
Don't wear tight pants
Don't wear pants at all
My father kicks me out of the nest
My mother keeps me in
Don't shout
Don't talk
Clean. Scrub. Arrange.
Don't expect praise
Don't fool around
Don't go out
Don't meet Rania
Rania's brother tried to propose to you
Don't talk to any girls while you're selling biscuits
Don't be long

Don't say no
It's time to get engaged
Don't stand on the balcony
Don't go to the dreams program
Don't go late by yourself to the pharmacy
even if you're sick
Don't talk to your friends
Don't worry it's a regular visit
Don't fight it, the razor
Wake up
Don't cry, he needed to cut it off
Don't look for it
It would have made you crazy
and out of control.

My father hates girls
He says they used to bury them
when they were born.
No value
No personality
This is not your house
You can't go out
Clean. Scrub. Arrange.
Don't imagine more
Don't stand on the balcony
Don't lose your virginity
Don't look from the window
My mother keeps me in
My father kicks me out

My brother beats me up
The doctor cuts me off
Don't. Don't.

I want to read
so I can read the Koran
read the signs in the street
know the number of the bus
I'm supposed to take
when I one day leave this house.

WOULD YOU RATHER (I)

(*Darkness. Two girls lying on the floor, only a flashlight.*)

GIRL 1

Would you rather be alone or be with a guy who stutters?

GIRL 2

Why do you always want to do this?

GIRL 1

Just answer. Would you rather be with someone famous who dumps you or never be with someone famous at all? Would you rather be called a slut or fat?

GIRL 2

This is a stupid game.

GIRL 1

Just answer.

GIRL 2

They're stupid questions.

GIRL 1

Would you rather be blind, deaf, or dumb?

GIRL 2

None of the above.

GIRL 1

Would you rather get pregnant accidentally or get dumped?

GIRL 2

Usually they happen at the same time.

GIRL 1

Would you rather be called a dyke or a bitch?

GIRL 2

Dyke, definitely.

GIRL 1

Okay, I'll give you a nice one 'cause you answered. Would you rather be the most brilliant or most beautiful?

GIRL 2

Both.

GIRL 1

Pick one.

GIRL 2

Most sarcastic.

GIRL 1

Would you rather get HPV or give HPV?

GIRL 2

Ew!

GIRL 1

Answer!

STEPHANIED

I was raised Catholic
I found Christ
Then I found Stephanie
I always find a good thing
Then I find something better.
I'm not gay
I'm not straight
I'm Stephanied.
I didn't do anything if she didn't do it
I played house with her
I held her hand all the time
Everyone disappeared from my world
She wore jelly sandals
She had long black hair
She hated kickball
I hated kickball
She loved super-cinnamon gum
I loved it too

Once when I was in her bedroom
I snuck into her drawers
I stole her T-shirt
It was soft and it smelled like her
Nothing was good unless she liked it
Nothing was fun unless she wanted to do it with me
She said you have to give your money to anyone who needs it
She said it was important to rehearse for dying
We used to lie still and hold our breath
She said we should practice kissing
She told me to put my tongue in her mouth
It tastes better when you take your time
She said you can only love someone
if they're your friend.
I'm not gay
I'm not straight
I'm Stephanied.

GIRL FACT

Research has shown that girls involved with sports in high school are less likely to engage in risky sexual behaviors such as high numbers of partners, inconsistent or no use of birth control, or engaging in sex while under the influence of drugs or alcohol.

The decrease in girls' participation in risky sexual behavior associated with sports involvement is partly due to a delay in sexual initiation and partly to social-psychological dynamics such as enhanced self-confidence, a less stereotypically feminine gender role identity, and/or a stronger desire to avoid teenage pregnancy.

MOVING TOWARD THE HOOP

There is a whistle
and I know I am supposed
to move go begin dribble
Whistle
The ball hot in my hands
burns
The clock is on
I begin my journey down the court
down this alley in my brain
Each game
I weave from end to end
It's not the other girls
who are in my way
I am fast
I have the moves
There are far more deadly obstacles
that keep me from the hoop
Blind pass

She passes back
Crossover dribble
They are double-teaming me
at the intersection
Color
Girl
Girl
Color
Ganging up on my consciousness
Not sure in which court I stand
or if I'm either one
or both
or something else
like poor
or maybe all
or maybe none
or maybe
just ball burning in my hands
just weaving darting dribbling
down the court
Each basket defies what is expected
because nothing is
even though they expect us to play ball
but not me
not girl
even if I'm tall

Which part of me do I ally myself with?
Which part do I ignore?

At what moment?

Which part doesn't belong?

Which group will it piss off?

Which group do I represent?

I am an athlete

A girl with strong legs

and arms

I train

I am also the child

of a Dominican mother

and a black father

so I am black

well brown

brown and black

Canela

Morena

Indian

and girl

Weave cross

What goes between

What stories

What past

What ropes around my neck

What scholarship

What affirmative action plan

What resentful boys in my hood

What champions

What being best

What talk show hosts

What Spanish French U.S. invaders
of our land
What ho
What manly arms
What nappy-headedness
What muscled ugly lesbian
What never get a man
What postracial
biracial
nonracial
multiracial
I almost trip and stumble over ball

What land they stole
What bodies in chains
What indigenous Taino people they killed with their
white diseases
What Indians
What Africans
What women bound and raped
What legs
What race
have I been running
What identity have I been ducking
or too defiantly embracing
What president
What civil rights leaders dead
What country
What team

What right do I have?

Who do I think I am?

What legacy that never ends?

What Katrina

What Jena Six

What Detroit, Watts, Lower Ninth, South Bronx,

Soweto, Kibera, Eastland,

favela, Dharavi, barrio

What eastern Congo

What prisons

What brothers

who could have been

dribbling

Who am I

girl

to take their place?

Pass now

Weave

Think

What future

What opportunities

Must win

Must get control

Fake

Duck

Lay up

Overcome

Break open
Free of guards
In possession
Dunk
Score

SOPHIE ET APOLLINE

or, Why French Girls Smoke

SOPHIE

    I started at a party

    I wanted to join in

    I wanted to do what everyone was doing

    At the beginning I didn't want to smoke

    all the time

APOLLINE

    I am anxious about the future

    My studies

    Work

    It is very expensive

    How will I ever live in Paris?

    How will I find something I like to do?

    I smoke to avoid the future

SOPHIE

I smoke when I'm not happy
I smoke when I'm sad about my friends
and family
When they lie, when they betray me

APOLLINE

Sophie is my best friend
We share a lot of things
We are supporting each other
We don't like the same people
We don't like the same girls
The ones who are really self-confident
and put the other girls down
One group totally popular the other not

SOPHIE

We are not popular
You have to talk loud
You have to be the center of attention
Popular girls smoke for style

APOLLINE

Unpopular girls smoke for stress

SOPHIE

My mother is a closet smoker
She hides like me
She thinks I don't see her.

APOLLINE

My father thinks his daughter is the perfect
    girl
That means good results at school
No boyfriends
No sex
No smoking
No drugs
First time I had sex I was sixteen
It was very bad
The boy wasn't my boyfriend
Just a friend
I didn't want to have sex
I was a little drunk
I regret that he wasn't the boy I liked
I am with my boyfriend now
He is gentle. He pays attention to me.
We have sex one or two times a week.

SOPHIE

The first time I was with a boy I didn't know
It was very good
He cared about me
He said he wasn't a virgin
but I think he was
He was shy and didn't know what he was doing
He was kind with me
I talk to my father about sex

He asks me questions
He asks if it is good for me and
what we did.
Sometimes I don't answer
He says I have to be careful
Don't get pregnant and diseases

APOLLINE

I wish my parents knew I had a boyfriend
They wouldn't approve so I don't tell them

SOPHIE

I like the way I look, the way my hand moves when I smoke.
    I feel more confident and grown up.

APOLLINE

The good future:
A wonderful job
A family, three children, two boys and a girl
I always wanted two brothers, one older, one younger
I wanted to take care of the younger
    and wanted the older to take care of me.

SOPHIE

The good future:
I want to have money
I want to play in the theater

I want a girl because she's cute. She will be a princess.
Beautiful clothes. No problems.

APOLLINE

Bad future:
People don't care about other people
They only care about themselves
People sleep in the streets
A lot of poor

SOPHIE

Teenagers do bad things.
Drugs and fight
They don't realize reality
They are in a dream
They only care about themselves
and no one else

APOLLINE

I can talk to Sophie
She is my best friend
I can laugh with her
When I'm sad I know she will be there
for me

SOPHIE

I can be myself with Apolline
She won't judge me

I know it's bad to smoke
but I don't think I'm an addict

APOLLINE

I know I'm an addict
I will stop when my studies finish
Peut-être

THINGS I HEARD ABOUT SEX

It's loud and scary

My mother and father were doing it once

in the next room

I thought my mother was dying

It can kill you

It can free you

Just say no

You can'say no

You won't want to say no

It's natural

It's healthy

It's evil

Boys want it more than girls

Girls want it more than boys

Guys don't know what they're doing

Only allowed to do it when you are making babies

My mother says it's spiritual

I wish my mother wouldn't say anything

Know your vagina
It's yours
Ask questions
Practice abstinence
Get birth control
It can take you over
You can catch dirty things
Bleeding makes you want it
Bleeding is the beginning
It can ruin you
Consume you
Masturbating is important
Masturbating is illegal
Sex is only about love
Sex is another sport like gymnastics

It makes you lose weight
360 calories an hour.

I DANCE (I)

Heart

Beat

Sound

Move

Make

Shake

Body

Want

Girl

Hips

Girl

Feet

Girl

Ground

Girl moving now

I dance to disappear
I dance to know I'm here
I dance 'cause I'm horny
'Cause it's holy
'Cause I want to forget

I dance 'cause I'm pissed off
I dance 'cause I can't
study anymore
I dance 'cause it's better
than sexting
R u naked?
What r u doing with ur hands?

I dance because everything is possible
I dance 'cause it gets me high
'Cause it's the one thing
you can't take away
I dance 'cause it keeps me
separate
from everyone else's
opinions and ideas
I dance 'cause I'm
bleeding
bleeding
becoming

I dance 'cause I can touch
the music

in the discos of Reykjavik
Mumbai, Manhattan, Barcelona
I dance till my mascara
runs down my chin

I dance to the drums of the forest and rivers
I dance to the beat of the cicadas
I dance to the traffic
to the crowds
to the silence
I dance to the end of unkindness
I dance past the killing fields
I dance past Wounded Knee
I dance past the skeletons and bones
I dance past slave branding
and Holocaust tattoos
I dance past inflicted identities
and demeaning looks
I dance past the limited determinations of my
abilities and worth
I dance past your lustful eyes
Your dirty interpretations of my teenage body
I shake off the burqas and bindings
and corsets and diets
I shake off restrictions and illegitimate rules
I shake off your suffocating warnings
I dance to the heartbeat of life
I dance because girls are the ultimate survivors

Section II

I BUILD IT WITH STONE

I make altars everywhere
I wear 16 bracelets on my arm
I write your name in red felt tip pen on my pillowcase
I wallpaper your posters above my bed
I engrave your initials on my closet door
I get to the stable 2 hours early so
I can brush your brown shiny coat 125 times
I run 6 more miles without stopping
I only wear sky-blue socks
I practice chords until my fingers cannot bend
I tattoo 56 stars on the right side of my face
I fast for Ramadan
I hand out every flyer for peace in Sudan
I memorize Hebrew
I memorize for the open slam
I collect 100 glass horses
I chant my mantra at dawn
I don't step on the cracks

I don't eat meat
I hold my breath when the light is red
I stay awake for 3 days
I learn anorexia
I do jump shots for 7 hours
I compulsively practice Latin
Latine loqui coactus sum

I read every poem
I recite every word
I watch every film
I know your every move
I play your video and I memorize every step you make
I receive your tweets
I know your pain
I sing your songs
I make you presents out of twigs and shells and feathers
I put them at the foot of the stage
I scream when the lights come up
I call you and hang up 7 times
I know you can see my ID number
I am searching
for mother
for answers
for a reason
for tomorrow
for God
for Allah
for more

for less
for my teacher Mrs. Martin
for everything
for nothing

I bow down
I pierce
I starve
I smoke marijuana
I go to church
I sing louder
I call your name
I stay in the water
I cut off my hair
I grow it long
I get on my knees
I build it with stone
Devoted.

GIRL FACTS

When a group of children who were interviewed
on *20/20* were asked if they'd rather be fat or
lose an arm, they unanimously answered
that they'd rather lose an arm.

The mortality rate associated with anorexia
nervosa is twelve times as high as the death rate
of *all* causes of death for females aged
fifteen to twenty-four.

hunger blog

i don't really like celery. tastes like disappointment. egg whites
taste like baby skin. learning to graze. used to watch cows. they
move their mouth around the grass. hover, hang, munch a little,
rest. don't swallow too much.

everyone's mad at me. here's a picture of my hips. bone jutting.
love those two words: bone jutting. just right for jeans. sade,
sexy music, and espresso help a lot. perfect combo. slow music
and caffeine annihilate hunger.

bad taste in my mouth. this girl jewel said i was sick in gym class.
she's jealous. last night i ate cooked vegetables naked in front of
the mirror. it grossed me out so much i haven't been hungry for
almost 24 hrs.

BLOG 4

everything sucks. had to stay home from school. too tired. dad
gave me a big lecture. said i wasn't fooling anyone. tried to exer-
cise. only got through a hundred sit-ups. watched tv. saw this
program about hundreds of people in Africa forced to leave their
land 'cause of war. they were drinking dirty water. everyone was
so hungry and sick. my mother was crying. she said i look just
like them. she made me soup. wanted to share it with the people
on tv. i like soup.

BLOG 5

can't stop crying. disgust myself. family forced me to eat a meal
'cause it's christmas eve. now i'm gross. putrid. foul. holidays
make me so sad. we're not happy like everyone else. always feel
there is something i should be doing, somewhere i should be
going. don't know where that is. maybe santa claus will leave
me diet pills under the tree. had christmas nightmares.
dreamed my family was making me eat reindeer meat. there
were sad antlers on my plate. then i was trying to run in really
deep snow and it turned to jello and i was happy 'cause jello
is a safe food but it turned out it was radioactive and i was
going to die.

BLOG 6

i believe in splenda. i like all substitutes. even miss hammer
who only teaches on occasion. she never makes me feel bad. i
can tell she was really skinny once 'cause she's got wrinkles like
that. she asked me what i felt like when i was thin. empty, not
full of bad stuff.

BLOG 7

my doctor said he is going to sue me for malpractice to my own body. he was gentle the way he examined me. i got so cold and was shivering. exciting to see bone. like finally getting to water after digging for years. almost pretty.

BLOG 8

was sent to an eating disorder clinic. today we planted a tree in the yard, which symbolized our bodies growing healthy. i like my roommate china a lot. she has a tattoo of a hamburger on her ass. a reminder. reimagining our bodies in art therapy. i saw myself as a belly dancer with sparkly shaking bells and things. it was good for about two hours. then i got really depressed. beautiful is a country with gates around it. i'll never be invited.

BLOG 9

the therapist just doesn't understand. its not like i think about it, okay? it lives there. must be thin. logo stenciled across my con-sciousness. like a permanent demand, like a mental coffee stain. maybe the whole system will just crash and they'll have to program me with something else. shrink asks what would that be? i don't know. annoying shrink asks again. okay, okay. maybe new logo reads: must not hurt so much. must be MORE PROFOUND. must be easy. must not be about only me. must not take up all this time. must not make me feel left out. MUST NOT MAKE ME WANT TO KILL MYSELF. i think i sound angry. everyone is really quiet for a long time. then china says maybe there's no more logos or de-mands. maybe we just make it up as we go and so there's no pres-sure or point. we're just here, okay. with each other, doing stuff.

THE JOKE ABOUT MY NOSE

Tehran, Iran

I was funny once. Really funny. Like everything I did and said funny. You would probably be laughing right now. I wish you were laughing. I wish I could give you examples of the funny I once was, but then I would still be funny. I know it's hard to believe looking at me now. I look so pretty, right? Aren't I pretty? Pretty girls don't really look like anything particular. They look like everyone dreams of looking, but they do not look like anything you can really identify. When you describe someone pretty you say things like, "Oh, that girl, Ashley, she's so pretty." But when you describe not so pretty girls you always say something special about them, something about how they look. Oh, Maria, she's the one with the wild hair, or Taina, her legs are a little short but she has great breasts.

Before when I was funny I looked funny. I looked like something unexpected about to happen. It all had to do with my nose. It was big and ugly and funny. My nose was funny. When you met me you met my nose. Hi, welcome to my nose. I wouldn't even say I had a face. Just nose. Just big funny ridiculous nose. Noses are so intense. I mean have you ever really looked at yours? I used to look at mine all the time. It fascinated me. God, what is a nose? Even the word is so funny. Nose. The idea of nose.

My nose put everyone at ease. It was a conversation breaker. Somehow it let everyone know I could be trusted. It is hard to describe, but my nose gave me permission. It inspired me with wicked ideas. It made me daring. It was like you'll never be one of them so you might as well be yourself. I was the one in my classes who was the clown. They called me Gonzo. Like the muppet.

My parents are not bad people. I know they love me. I know they want what's best for me. But that involves their idea of what is best. And it has meant they know better than me. My parents who loved me planned, strategized, and eventually succeeded at killing my nose. Murdering it.

On my sixteenth birthday they paid a man to take my nose out. They hired a hit man to take my poor nose down. The only problem is that my nose was attached to me.

I didn't even know what was happening. They kept telling me I would be happy and everything would be better and I would thank them for it because my life would be so much easier. I thought they were taking me to Paradise Chang restaurant. I thought we were going to have my favorite Chinese food. Then we were at this little hospital clinic place. I didn't understand. There was a doctor who oddly had a big nose himself. He told me it was a really simple procedure. My mother looked guilty, but she kept making herself smile. Then the doctor drugged me. I don't remember anything. When I woke up I was so nauseous and they were all hovering strangely over me and I could tell something terrible had happened. I started vomiting flesh and bone and blood. My nose was coming out all over me, ruined hammered destroyed. I was crying and I didn't even really know how to cry without a nose. And my father took my hand and said, "You will be a princess now," and I said, "I don't want to be a princess. I was happy being a clown. My nose protruded but it gave me history and mystery. It made me what I was. There is nothing now. Just this stupid mess in the middle of my face. I was once Mesopotamia and now I'm a mall."

I know this is hard to believe but I never dreamed of being pretty. I felt sorry for the pretty girls 'cause everyone was always staring at them. They never really talked or did anything. They were just there, like . . . pretty. Goldfish in a bowl. Just swimmering around, being looked at. Occasionally nibbling at the fish food, but nibbling 'cause we all know skinny is the same as pretty. That's the thing about being pretty. There are so many things you have to not do to be pretty. I mean it becomes your life. Not doing things. I stay pretty. I do pretty. I don't eat. I pick. I circle. I visit. I deprive. I starve. Because I do not eat, I do not have much energy. Food actually makes your brain function. So pretty people move slower. They can't do too much. They do not have very expansive thoughts. But then again, they don't need to. They're pretty.

Funny people can eat all they want. I used to love food. You can enjoy it 'cause funny people enjoy everything.

Pretty people mainly hang out with other pretty people. That's sort of what they do. Then it's all about who is prettier. Your whole life becomes about being the prettiest.

I miss my nose. Every day I rub it and dream of telling lies like Pinocchio so it will grow back. I went on this secret date with a boy who told me I was pretty. I'm not really. He thought I was being coy. I wasn't born pretty. I'm not naturally pretty. I'm fake pretty. He didn't understand and so he kissed me 'cause that's what boys do when they don't know something and don't want to look stupid. When he kissed me there was nothing in the way. It was too easy. I didn't even have to make a joke about it. And that was sad 'cause the joke about my nose always made the guy laugh and then we both relaxed and kissing was always so much better then.

WOULD YOU RATHER (II)

GIRL 1

Would you rather get caught stealing or cheating? Would you rather ask him to put on a condom or give him oral sex?

GIRL 2

I don't want to play this.

GIRL 1

Would you rather lose your mother or your father? Be in a tsunami or an earthquake? Be buried alive or freeze to death?

GIRL 2

I'm going to sleep.

GIRL 1

Why won't you ever play?

(*Silence*)

It's just a game.

(*Silence*)

You're no fun.

GIRL FACT

About one in three high school students have
been or will be involved in an abusive
relationship. Forty percent of teenage girls ages
fourteen to seventeen say they know someone
their age who has been hit or beaten
by a boyfriend.

Dear Rihanna,

I used to really respect you. I even got your haircut, all cute and straight shaggy shaped even though I have blonde hair. It looks better on you. I thought you were a caring and compassionate girl singer artist so I just don't understand why you were so mean to Chris. I see the way he looks at you. He just loves you too much. You know that. How could you dump him after one bad thing? It's so shallow to drop someone after they mess up. You have everything, Rihanna. You're perfect pretty and mega talented and sparkly and shiny. It must be hard for Chris to be with you. I mean I'm jealous of you and you're not even my girlfriend. Everyone wants you. Everyone wants to be you. In his apology video Chris seemed so nervous and sad. People say he was just reading his lines, but they were heartfelt. He was so scared about screwing up. He was so sad. I could tell. That's what happens after. I mean they feel so bad. They don't have anyone to help them. They don't know how to talk. I mean I can tell he wants to cry. Take him back. He loves you too much, but at least he loves you. One mistake you can't just fire him. What if he did that to you? Chris made you a video and put it out in front of the whole world. That's a lot to do in front of his friends and stuff. My boyfriend, Brad, didn't make me a video. I mean once he brought me this bracelet with a silver heart after he made my lip bleed. But he's never been as nice as Chris. My mother hates him. Brad, that is. She just doesn't know him. She judges him by one aspect of his personality but that's only a part of who he is. I heard Oprah say if a boy hits you once, leave 'em right then, but that's so cold, so mechanical. Like push boy delete.

I don't know about you, but I'm not perfect. I'm naggy and I complain, well that's what Brad tells me. I make him feel bad. I mean you shoved Chris and threw away his keys. That's serious for a boy. A guy's keys are like his self. I know if I did that I would be expecting a confrontation and you really shouldn't dish it out if you can't take it. We're all part of this. You can't even really say where it begins or ends. It's like my parents' arguments. They feel like they've been going on since I was born and they basically are always pissed off about the same things and she makes him feel so bad about himself and then he gets ugly. And sometimes he hurts her and then she gets meaner and we all just go to our rooms and pretend we don't hear, but really we're all part of it. I mean sometimes it's one of us that makes them start arguing. Usually me. My dad says someone's always asking for it.

Chris loves you. Just like Brad loves me. He knows me better than anyone. It's just sometimes this thing goes off in them. It's like all the hurt they feel and all the bad things they've seen and all the ways they couldn't help. I mean Chris used to wet his bed after his stepdad hit his mother. What are we gonna do, throw all the boys away? Put them forever on some punishment island? Then how are we gonna have babies? And who's gonna kiss us?

They're all crazy sad you know. I can tell even when Brad slaps me sometimes. It doesn't hurt as much as seeing how alone he is and confused and sad. My dad has that same sadness and it makes me smoke when I think about it. It really rips me apart.

Brad isn't buying your music anymore. He said if you were his girlfriend he would have to keep you locked up in his room. He couldn't bear everyone staring at you and dreaming about you. That made me a little jealous. I mean he doesn't let me out much and if I talk to another boy he gets real crazy, but the way he talked about you was different. Like he really had it for you. So imagine what poor Chris feels with so many guys everywhere having it for you. How is some guy gonna handle that? Most of the time they can't even find a good job. Well, Chris had one. But most guys my age are tripping about what they're gonna do. You're so strong, Rihanna. I watch you in the videos. Your arms and the way you move and your confidence. You look right into the camera. You are so much stronger. You could help Chris. Otherwise how are these boys gonna keep up? It's like when we're on the lake and I look at the water behind our motorboat and there's this wake and it stays there after the boat has passed. There's just these light waves of where something was once. It fills me with dread and makes me really scared. Sometimes I stop breathing. It's like none of us were ever really here at all. I don't want to be looking back on Brad like that. He's the one real thing.

GIRL FACT

Girls between thirteen and eighteen years of age
constitute the largest group in the sex industry.
It is estimated that around half a million girls
below the age of eighteen are victims of
trafficking each year.

I HAVE 35 MINUTES BEFORE HE COMES LOOKING FOR ME

Sofia, Bulgaria

I am sixteen.
I am trembling.
I am always trembling.
The trembling is like
a body flinching after
it's been shot.
I am dead
inside.

He will come back.
I must speak quickly.
I hate my hair.
I was sold two years ago.
I can't get out.
I am meat.
I am an animal.

I am sixteen.

I am owned by them.

They do what they want.

I am tall.

My legs are long.

There are burns.

I am an ashtray.

A garbage pail.

My hands trembling.

Sometimes they refuse to use condoms.

If we refuse them, we are beaten.

Look my back

There are gashes

I was twelve.

My father always drunk.

Always angry.

His friend, his best friend

who was forty

started raping me.

Whenever he saw me.

He threatened to ruin me

if I told.

He threatened to tell my father.

Two years

I did what he wanted.

He gave me syphilis.

This is herpes on my mouth.

I hate my hair.

(*She stands up.*)

What, what?

Are you sure he doesn't know?

Are you sure he isn't coming in?

(*She sits down.*)

We got caught. My father's
best friend. Someone walked
in when he was raping me
against a wall.
He told my father I put him
up to it.
My father believed him.
My father beat me with a
wooden piece of furniture
and threw me out.
I could not walk for weeks.
But I was on the run.

17 minutes

My father exiled me,
and my mother,
because she was with him
twenty-two years,
did not speak up.
Fourteen, no place to go,
on the streets,
a man took me in.
Then my brother
my only friend

turned his back on me.
Then the man started
beating . . .

No place to go.
No way out.
Next to the police
Went there for help
A stolen wallet
A young one with a
crew cut
told me he knew of a job.
He brought me in. He sold me to them.
If I try to leave
they will kill my family.
I still love them.
The police
tied me to a bed
for seven hours
handcuffed my hands
made me naked
and six of them . . .
I am a garbage pail.
I am a receptacle.
I have been sick
There is no time
5 minutes
I don't know why I was born.
I do not feel pleasure

I am only vulgar
Only flesh
If someone could see my heart
they would see it isn't there

I hate my hair
I haven't heard from
my mother in a year
This is not a choice
You go to the police to protect
You go to
Your father
Your mother
Your brother
Your boyfriend
I am sixteen
I am an animal
I am property
I am a receptacle
I am trembling
I am found on the streets of Paris
I am Bulgarian
I am from the Philippines
I was taken from Sierra Leone
I am Russian
I am from the killing fields
Sold in Tel Aviv, Amsterdam, Atlanta
I'm from Kosovo, Bombay, Ghana, Lebanon
I am a raped opening

I am about to become extinct
There will be nothing left of me
    Elephant
    Eagle
    Girl

GIRL FACT

Barbie was based on a German doll called Lilli
that was sold as a sexy novelty for men.

FREE BARBIE

Kwai Yong, China

Hello, my name is Chang Ying. I wish I could write you a proper letter, but I'm in a factory and I work twelve hours a day and if I'm late or I complain they will throw me out. Even thinking these thoughts could get me in trouble 'cause I could mess up and get my hand caught in the machine.

They hate it when we hurt the machines. They hate it when anything happens to us 'cause it slows everything down. That's how LiJuan died. There was a fire one day and she was scared to leave her station 'cause she needed the job to feed her family and she was burned too badly.

But I can't lie, I couldn't really write you a letter 'cause I can't read. I'm thirteen and I have been working since I was a kid. I speak good Chinese, I just can't write it or read it.

But I have a lot to say and I think I can help you.

You may not think some poor girl who only makes a few cents an hour has anything to teach you. But I know a lot about

Barbie. I am one of the people who makes her head. I actually see what goes into it.

As you can tell by now I have found a way to get this message to you. It isn't a letter or Internet or phone. It's what I call *Head Send.* Can you feel it? It is very strong. I started doing it when I was five. You have to think a thought very very intensely and then you have to imagine someone receiving the thought and then you close your eyes and concentrate and your head sends it.

Because I make Barbie's head I *Head Send* my thoughts into each one of her brains. So whatever girl gets her will hear my thoughts.

I have made many, many heads so my message is in a lot of places. If you listen very closely to your Barbie—put her head to your ear like a shell—you will hear what I have to say.

Many, many of us girls are needed to make Barbie because three Barbies are sold every second. They told us this the first day of the job. They said girls like me were working in a lot of countries to make Barbie perfect. Her body comes from Taiwan. Her hair gets stuck on in Japan. Then she comes to China to get clothes and get her head put on her body. They said that 23,000 trucks a day go back and forth to the harbor crammed with Barbies so they can all sail to America and get packaged in pink and sent out.

They told us what we did here in China was the most important part and that we had to do it fast or we would not keep up and then little girls couldn't get their Barbies.

At the beginning I used to worry about this and I would always be very nervous. I cut my hand a few times in the machine.

Then I saw a picture of Barbie's dream house and it made me start thinking about where I live. I live in a nightmare house. It's not even a house, a dormitory. It's like prison Barbie, all us girls shoved into one ugly place. I started thinking about how one Barbie costs 200 yuan, but I work here where it is so hot, all day, six days a week, and I don't make that much in a whole week.

I have never been anywhere else but I do not think anyone really looks like Barbie. She is so skinny, I heard she can't even get her period. And my cousin who lives in America told me that Barbie makes the girls who own her stop eating because they try and look like her.

I started thinking about how it's actually hard to love Barbie the way she is now. She is very tough, so much plastic. She's not cuddly at all. She can't even put her arms around you. You have to do things for her: worship her, dress her, buy her things. She wants everything. She is very greedy and needy. That's how they get you to spend more money.

Listen, it's not Barbie's fault, she doesn't even have a chance. So many people control her—from the first plastic mold to her final accessory. In many ways she has less freedom than even me. She has no ability to walk away. Her legs probably wouldn't hold her up anyway. So many people abuse her. You know, there is a whole group of Barbies—here at the factory we secretly call them the unfortunate ones—they get sent to Barbie headquarters in Los Angeles and a room of Barbie experts throw them and kick them and bite them to see if they can take it.

My cousin also told me that many girls love their Barbie at the beginning and then when they get older they turn on her.

They cut off all her hair or even her head or put her in the microwave oven.

The people who are in charge make her say really stupid things. They put words in her mouth:

Will we ever have enough clothes?
I want to go shopping.
Math is hard.

I know Barbie doesn't really want to say any of this 'cause I know what's going on in her head. She talks to me. She's really angry. She's really hurting. She is really guilty. She hates shopping and feels bad about all the girls who are starved to make her and are starving to be like her. She's actually very messy and surprisingly loud. She is not at all polite and she hates being shoved into really tight clothes and pointy high uncomfortable shoes.

Barbie isn't who you think she is. She's so much smarter than they will let her be. She's got great powers and is kind of a genius.

There are more than a billion Barbies in the world. Imagine if we freed them. Imagine if they came alive in all the villages and cities and bedrooms and landfills and dream houses. Imagine if they went from makeover to takeover. Imagine if they started saying what they really felt.

Let Barbie speak.

Head Send:
Free Barbie!

Head Send:

Free Barbie!

Free Barbie!

Free Barbie!

Ow! I just got my hand caught! It hurts. It's bleeding. They are going to be very angry.

Head Send:

Free Chang Ying!

Head Send:

Free Chang Ying!

Let her out of this dirty sweaty factory.

Head Send:

Please.

SKY SKY SKY

Ramallah, Palestine

Dear Khalid,
I keep touching my hair
A kind of pastime
Running through
Running through.
It was thicker before.
Now it is water.
Something has left me.
I am not sure what it is.

Dear Khalid,
When I stood by your grave
I imagined them assembling
the pieces of your body like a puzzle.
Always this missing piece
and your hand

I kept thinking about your hand
gripping mine when you believed
in something enough
to die.
You would get excited.
Not happy excited like receiving a present.
More like determined.
No one was going to take your future
away from you.
I kept thinking about the pieces
of your body
and how I loved each piece
but never separated before like this.

Dear Khalid,
Later I realized it began as a fever, the rage.
Two weeks after they threw the dirt on you
and gave me the scarf you wore for good luck.
I thought it was one of those illnesses
that we get from the bad water
from the lack of light
when there is no bread
when there is no baby's milk
when everything gets shut down and off
when we are forced into one broken room for weeks,
months sometimes.
I thought it was an illness.
I was burning and I could not stop.
I wrapped myself in the fabric of your scarf

in your smell
thinking it would hold me in
or keep things out
but it didn't.

Dear Khalid,
It was simple
the voice
when it came to me
so perfect, so clear:
Suicide bomber.
I said it out loud
in front of my friends
in the café
and the fever finally broke.

Dear Khalid,
They told me not to think about it.
They told me I'd be a hero.
They told me I'd join you in paradise.
They spoke too quickly.
They moved too fast.
I needed to take time.
There was a boy who would go with me.
I could tell he was afraid.
He was sweating.
He had acne.
Someone or something had sent him there
and like me he was trying to catch up.

Dear Khalid,
Maybe if they had sent a car that had lights
or a car that wasn't broken or rusty.
Maybe if they hadn't rushed me so fast.
Maybe if they had let me dress like myself
but the idea of dying
in a tank top with my belly exposed
the idea of dying in their jeans
the way they were rough and squeezed me in . . .

Dear Khalid,
It could have been your baby
I was carrying against my skin
strapped on like that
sucking life out of me
but it was a bomb
the size of a torso
extending now, like an overgrown tumor
sucking the life
there could have been
little fingers instead of nails
something
we created out of tenderness
but it was something to blow
people up.

Dear Khalid,
In the plaza
where they play backgammon

we were sent to our places
like we were bad in school
to stand
to get ready to explode, to die
in our places.
I knew the boy wanted to turn back
but he was a boy and had no choice.
Then suddenly the plaza became
faces
faces, faces.
My mother, my father, my aunt, and you,
Khalid, were there in those Israeli plaza
eyes.
I looked up then
It was blue
Life-giving blue blue sky
bigger than the plaza
or Palestine or the Jews
or even you, Khalid.
There was sky sky sky
and I couldn't do it
and I turned as his body exploded
his boy head
shattered and now
there were more missing pieces.

Dear Khalid,
I do not understand why
they are keeping me here.

I changed my mind.

I turned back.

You would think they'd appreciate me.

You would have to imprison every Palestinian

for having bad fantasies or thoughts.

How else would we survive?

I don't really mind being in prison.

At least I no longer have to pretend I'm free.

I do not have illusions.

I do not have hate.

I do not have a boyfriend.

I cannot go home again,

I am older.

My hair is water.

THE WALL

Jerusalem, Israel

My friend Adina takes me to the other side of
the West Bank wall.
I am surprised at what it's like over there.
It somehow seems taller
You would need a helicopter to get over it
Hard mean cement dividing energy, houses,
land, and friends
I go back.
I hear more stories.
No water on this side,
No wells
No pomegranates or figs
No jobs
No way out.
I protest on Fridays
with mainly Palestinian boys.

They do not understand what an Israeli
girl is doing there.

It is a secret.
No one in my family knows.
This goes on for months.

The wall changes me.
I stop shaving my legs.
I stop eating meat.
Eventually I refuse to join the army.
I see the heartbreak in my grandfather's
tender old face.
I am told I am not giving back.
I am told I am not a real Israeli.
My father will not look at me
the way he did.
My older brother gets louder
and brags in my face
that he killed an Arab today.
I still say no.
I refuse to agree that I have mental problems.
I will not learn to shoot a gun.
I go to jail.
I refuse to wear the army/prison uniform.
I am put in solitary
I do not say how much this scares me.
Each night
a girl my age, eighteen or so,

wanders into my cell.

Her head is shaved.

She is naked and hungry.

There is something she wants me to know.

Then she is choking.

Her bony hands

claw at the wall.

I can't tell if she is a dream

or a memory.

Haunting

or releasing me.

GIRL FACT

A new report says of the estimated 300,000
child soldiers around the world, about 40 percent
of them are girls. The girls are often front-line
fighters or used as porters or cooks.
Many are sexually abused.

A TEENAGE GIRL'S GUIDE TO SURVIVING
SEX SLAVERY

Bukavu, Democratic Republic of the Congo

I live in Bukavu, Democratic Republic of the Congo, but I think
this guide applies to any girl anywhere in the world.

People ask me all the time how I survived. It wasn't that I was
smarter or even stronger than anyone else. I didn't even know
what I was doing. It was just that something inside me couldn't
go along. My friends, they got taken at the same time as me. I
don't think we will ever get them back.

RULE 1. GET OVER THAT GIRL THING: "THIS CAN'T BE
    HAPPENING TO ME"

When it happens, and trust me it happens to thousands of us,
you will not believe it.

You will think, *These are just crazy soldiers fooling around. They
must be bored or something. They couldn't be hurting me, grabbing my
arms and legs all rough like this, throwing me into their truck.* Your
brain will start telling you things. *They are old enough to be my*

father. They know better than this. This will be confusing. It will make you feel stupid. It will make you feel like what is happening is not really happening. It will make you will feel like you did something wrong.

I watched my best friends—Alisa, Esther, and Sowadi. We were on holiday. We took the boat together from Bukavu to Goma. We were joking around a lot on the lake—Lake Kivu. It's a really huge lake. It takes five hours to cross it. We were drinking Fantas and making fun of Esther's big crazy hair. We were going to Goma to swim and hang out. We went shopping. Sowadi bought these gold shoes. I remember thinking I wanted them too, but I didn't want her to think I was copying her.

As we walked out of the store and down this street, it didn't seem real. We were just shopping and now these crazy soldiers . . . that's why they didn't run. I wanted to run, but I didn't want to leave them. When we tried to refuse, that's when we got how serious it was. One of the soldiers, the real big one, started beating Alisa and she was screaming. My best friends were all screaming and crying.

I got very quiet. That's what I do. I wasn't going to let those soldiers know anything. That leads to

RULE 2. NEVER LOOK AT HIM WHEN HE IS RAPING YOU
He will call your name in that grating, craving voice. He will beg you to look. He will turn your head with his big rough dirty hands. Never move your eyes to his. Close them if you have to. He is nothing. He isn't even there. He is a teeny tiny meaningless speck. He doesn't even exist.

RULE 3. BUILD A HOLE INSIDE YOURSELF AND CLIMB INTO IT

He will be on top of you. He will be old enough to be your father.
He will smell like the woods, alcohol, and marijuana. He will
hold his hand over your mouth. You are a virgin. You are only fifteen. He will remind you that no one is coming.

Imagine you are dancing. Think of your favorite song. Remember your mother braiding your hair. Feel her kindly roughly
braiding hands. Hear her calling your name, "Marta, Marta,
Marta."

RULE 4. NEVER EVER OPEN ANY DOOR TO HIM

Reject the food he brings you. Refuse to eat his stupid fish. Spit
on it. Tell him your family would never eat fish out of the water.
When in public he will want you to smile and act like a proper
wife even though he is married to someone else. Never smile.
Roll on the ground in the ugly expensive tailor-made *pange* he
brings you. Never laugh at his jokes. He will be shoving himself
into you. He will do this two or three times a day. It will not be
painful after the first twenty times. Your insides will no longer
belong to you. He will sometimes wear cologne. Beware. That
smell will make you sympathetic. Do not give way to it. You will
begin to feel something for him. It's natural after six months. It
is nothing more than habit or accident. It has nothing to do with
Claude. By the way, never use his name. Only refer to him as
"him" or "you." "*You*, move over. *You*, leave me alone."

RULE 5. HIS SADNESS IS NONE OF YOUR BUSINESS

Sometimes he will seem so sad. All the bad things he has seen
and done. You will feel bad for him. You will feel everything he

feels and doesn't feel. You have been his slave for almost two years. You will start to think there is no one else. This is your life. He will be the only person who ever loves you. When you start vomiting one morning, you will be sure he poisoned you. Then it will pass, and then it will happen again, and slowly you will realize you are pregnant with his baby. He will tell you if you even think of aborting it he will kill you. Refuse to take care of his baby.

RULE 6. IT DOESN'T MATTER IF YOU GET CAUGHT, BETTER TO
    DIE TRYING TO BE FREE

When the opportunity reveals itself, flee. Count on miracles. When you run, you will take your baby because deep down you know she's yours. You will take her clothes and nothing else.

You will start to run and your legs will be strong like a strong person's legs and you will think clearer and better than you have ever thought before and you will hear your mother calling "Marta, run run run" and you will make the bus at the exact right moment and you will not look out the window because you know the four bodyguards who have watched you like a hawk for two years are already there but you are in your hole and no one can see you and you will hide with your baby inside a wall in your cousin's house the place you would have stayed on your holiday and Claude will come with the four other soldiers and they will search and destroy everything and your baby will not cry and you will be invisible and the next day you will make it to the boat and as it is pulling out from shore you will not be breathing you will see him and the other men on the dock asking and looking for you and someone will point to the boat and you will know he has found you even though you are deep inside the hole. And the captain of the boat will suddenly be standing next to you and he will ask you one single question "How old are you?" and then you will talk as if it's the first time you've talked and you will be surprised at how loud and crazy your voice sounds and you will say things like "I am seventeen. He took me when I was fifteen. He raped me every day three times a day. He gave me diseases and made me pregnant. He stole our country's minerals, and my life. If you turn this boat back, I will throw myself into the lake. I will drown myself. I'll be okay dead as long as I never have to see him again. I will take his baby with me."

And the captain will put one hand on your shoulder and you will see a light in his eyes that you will identify as pity and he will not turn back.

RULE 7. DO NOT FEEL GUILTY ABOUT HOW HAPPY YOU FEEL WHEN YOU HEAR HE IS DEAD

After six months back at home in your beloved Bukavu you will run into two soldiers from the camp and they will be surprised at how well you look and they will tell you that Claude got killed and you will say "God did something good" and at that moment milk will pour into your breasts and you will love your baby.

I went on a vacation for two days.
I didn't come back for two years.

RULE 8. NO ONE CAN TAKE ANYTHING FROM YOU IF YOU DO NOT GIVE IT TO THEM

I DANCE (II)

I dance in the circles
that began in ancient Greece
In the circles that spin round the Balkans,
Africa, Ireland
I dance the hora

I dance in the circle of all those indigenous
I dance to say yes to my culture
I dance because my grandmother
and grandfather taught me
I dance so I don't forget
I dance because there is a bird in me
Sometimes it is a slow bird in my body
Sometimes it moves so fast
like a blue jay
You cannot stop one
even if you try to kill one
Hold a gun right on a blue jay.

They will fly fast like that
Out of your way
I wanted to dance the jingle dance
before I could even walk
I dance because I love to spin
The buckskin dance
all over my body
When you teach Indian children to dance
you teach them to be Indians

I dance to disappear
I dance to know I'm here
I dance 'cause I'm horny
'cause it's holy
'cause I want to forget

(Belly dancing)
I dance with my belly
the center of the power of the world

(Sufi dancing)
I dance Sufi
and I spin out
forever
out into the universe

(Hula, kabuki, hip-hop, Bollywood dancing)
I dance past what is forbidden
on O'te'a

Kabuki and rock and roll
Hip-hop and Bollywood

(Salsa and flamenco)
I dance salsa and flamenco

Section III

Section III

REFUSER

From the Lebanese mountains
to the Kenyan village of El Doret
we are practicing self-defense.
Versed in karate, tai chi, judo, and kung fu
we are no longer surrendering to our fate.

Now we are the ones who walk our girlfriends home from school.
And we don't do it with macho. We do it with cool.

Our mothers are the Pink Sari Gang
fighting off the drunken men
with rose-pointed fingers and sticks in
Uttar Pradesh.
The Peshmerga women
in the Kurdish mountains
with barrettes in their hair
and AK-47s instead of pocketbooks.

We are not waiting anymore to be taken and retaken.

We are the Liberian women sitting
in the African sun blockading the exits
till the men figure it out.

We are the Nigerian women
babies strapped to our backs
occupying the oil terminals of Chevron.
We are the women of Kerala
who refused to let Coca-Cola
privatize our water.
We are Cindy Sheehan showing up in Crawford without a plan.
We are all those who forfeited husbands boyfriends and dates
'cause we were married to our mission.
We know love comes from all directions and in many forms.
We are Malalai Joya, who spoke back to the Afghan Loya Jirga
and told them they were "raping warlords" and
she kept speaking even when they kept
trying to blow up her house.
And we are Zoya, whose radical mother was shot dead when Zoya
was only a child so she was fed on revolution, which was
stronger than milk.

And we are the ones who kept and loved our babies
even though they have the faces of our rapists.
We are the girls who stopped cutting ourselves to release the
pain

And we are the girls who refused to have our clitoris cut
and give up our pleasure.

We are:
Rachel Corrie, who wouldn't/couldn't move away from the
     Israeli tank.
Aung San Suu Kyi, who still smiles after years of not being able
     to leave her room.
Anne Frank, who survives now 'cause she wrote down her story.
And we are Neda Soltani, gunned down by a sniper in the streets
     of Tehran as she voiced a new freedom and way.

We are the women riding the high seas to offer
needy women abortions on ships.
We are women documenting the atrocities
in stadiums with video cameras underneath our burqas.
We are seventeen and living for a year in a tree
and lying down in the forests to protect wild oaks.
We are out at sea interrupting the whale murders.
We are freegans, vegans, trannies,
but mainly we are refusers.
We don't accept your world
your rules your wars
We don't accept your cruelty and unkindness.
We don't believe some need to suffer for others to survive
or that there isn't enough to go around
or that corporations are the only and best economic
arrangement.

And we don't hate boys, okay?
That's another bullshit story.

We are refusers
but we crave kissing.
We don't want to do anything before we're ready
but it could be sooner than you think
and we get to decide
and we are not afraid of what is pulsing through us.
It makes us alive.

Don't deny us, criticize us, or infantilize us.
We don't accept checkpoints, blockades, or air raids.
We are obsessed with learning.
On the barren tsunamied beaches of Sri Lanka
In the desolate and soggy remains of the Lower Ninth
We want school.
We want school.
We want school.

We know if you plan too long
nothing happens and things get worse and that
most everything is found in the action
and instinctively we get that the scariest thing
isn't dying, but not trying at all.

And when we finally have our voice
and come together
When we let ourselves gather the knowledge

When we stop turning on each other
but direct our energy toward what matters
When we stop worrying about
our skinny-ass stomachs or too-frizzy hair
or fat thighs
When we stop caring about pleasing
and making everyone so incredibly happy—
We got the Power.

If
Janis Joplin was nominated the ugliest man on her campus
and they sent Angela Davis to jail
If Simone Weil had manly virtues
and Joan of Arc was hysterical
If Bella Abzug was eminently obnoxious
and Ellen Johnson Sirleaf is considered scary
If Arundhati Roy is totally intimidating
and Rigoberta Menchú is pathologically intense
and Julia Butterfly Hill is an extremist freak
Call us hysterical then
Fanatical
Eccentric
Delusional
Intimidating
Eminently obnoxious
Militant
Bitch
Freak
Tattoo me

Witch
Give us our broomsticks
and potions on the stove
We are the girls
who are aren't afraid to cook.

GIRL FACT

An estimated one hundred million girls are involved in child labor worldwide.

WHAT DO YOU LIKE ABOUT BEING A GIRL?

Girls are kind
We get to be glamorous
You can wear makeup
Girls are human
Girls are close to their fathers
Girls don't force boys to do stuff
Girls wear pretty clothes
Girls can create a new life
Girls are shy
Girls are tender
Girls are soft
Boys sit for hours and never talk
They yell at the television
Girls can do things better
Ballet
Wearing dresses
Being different
Women are closer.

ASKING THE QUESTION

So we're lying there kissing and feeling each other up
and it's getting hotter and I can tell he thinks I'm not into it
'cause all I'm thinking about is how I'm going to ask him,
how I am going to say it.
I'll make him uptight.
He'll know I've done this before.
He'll think I'm a nerd.
I know all boys hate them.
It doesn't feel as good.
It breaks up the motion,
the momentum.
He won't call me again.
He'll feel bad, like something's wrong with him.
He's nervous already.
He'll lose it.
He couldn't have AIDS.
He's too young.
He's too handsome.

He's too athletic.
He's too nice.
He's too shy.
He's too funny.
He dresses too well.
He's too clean.
He's too smart.
He's too careful.
He's too popular.
He's too Christian.
I've known him my whole life.
Maybe I'll ask him the next time
when we know each other better.

Then I remember this girl in my class.
She was seventeen.
She was really cute.
She was going to marry this guy.
He didn't tell her he slept with
someone else.
He didn't tell her 'cause he
didn't want her to break up with him.
He didn't tell her
and she trusted him
and he gave her HIV.
So I say
just like that
"Would you mind
using a condom please?"

(I sound just like my mother)

and he says, without even missing a beat,

"Sure, I have one right here."

and I think

oh my God

that wasn't so bad.

Kind of easy

and he's clearly done this before.

So he's not that shy,

not so insecure,

clearly not a virgin,

clearly prepared.

Maybe I don't really know who he is.

I do that.

I make people up.

I make up what they think

and how they will respond.

I get so inside him

that I don't think about me.

Why didn't he bring it up?

Maybe he was going to put it on

at the last minute.

Maybe he has a way of doing it

so it doesn't stop the flow.

How many times has he done this?

How many girls has he slept with?

And he says, just like that,

"This is my first time,

I'm kind of awkward,"

and I start laughing
and he says, "Are you laughing at me?"
and I say, "No, I'm laughing 'cause
I'm awkward too and I'm happy
you're like me."
And we kiss some more
and then later he takes out the condom
and we laugh at it
'cause condoms are really funny looking
and it ends up being something
we do together
and we're both protecting ourselves
and each other
and this makes me like him
and me.

WOULD YOU RATHER (III)

GIRL 1

Would you rather catch your boyfriend sleeping with your best friend or your sister?

GIRL 2

Would you rather keep annoying me or let me sleep?

GIRL 1

Wow, you're so grumpy!

GIRL 2

Would you rather be someone I invite over again or keep asking really stupid questions?

GIRL 1

Why are you so upset?

GIRL 2

'Cause all your questions are totally depressing me.

'Cause I am sick of having to choose between two horrible impossible things.

Living with my mother or my father, being popular or smart, enjoying sex or being called a slut, making money or following my heart.

I want different questions. I hate these choices. I hate my life.

GIRL 1

I'm sorry. I'm so sorry. It was just a game.
(*Girl 2 is crying.*)

GIRL 1

Are you crying?

GIRL 2

Yes.
(*Pause, silence*)

GIRL 1

Would you rather I stay over here and let you alone or come there and snuggle up with you?

GIRL 2

The second.

GIRL 1

Come over there?

GIRL 2

Yeah.

(*She comes over and snuggles with her.*)

GIRL 1

I'm sorry.

GIRL 2

It's just so hard sometimes. It's just so hard and sad.

GIRL 1

I know. It is. I hate it.

(*They both snuggle and they both cry. Then after a while they start laughing and laughing.*)

THINGS I LIKE ABOUT MY BODY

Being big
My curves
Being petite, my own little shape
My eyes
My smile
My skin—caramel color, smooth and shiny
My Chinese eyes
Dimples—one is deeper
My hairy legs
Curly eyelashes
I like everything
Eyes like the sun
Arms like a stick
Tallness like a tree
Hairy like a monkey

MY SHORT SKIRT

My short skirt
is not an invitation
a provocation
an indication
that I want it
or give it
or that I hook.

My short skirt
is not begging for it
it does not want you
to rip it off me
or pull it up or down.

My short skirt
is not a legal reason
for raping me
although it has been before

it will not hold up
in the new court.

My short skirt, believe it or not,
has nothing to do with you.

My short skirt
is about discovering
the power of my calves
about cool autumn air traveling
up my inner thighs
about allowing everything I see
or pass or feel to live inside.

My short skirt is not proof
that I am stupid
or undecided
or a malleable little girl.

My short skirt is my defiance.
I will not let you make me afraid.
My short skirt is not showing off,
this is who I am
before you made me cover it
or tone it down.
Get used to it.

My short skirt is happiness.
I can feel myself on the ground.

I am here. I am hot.
My short skirt is a liberation
flag in the women's army.
I declare these streets, any streets,
my vagina's country.

My short skirt
is turquoise water with swimming colored fish
a summer festival in the starry dark
a bird calling
a train arriving in a foreign town.
My short shirt is a wild spin
a full breath
a tango dip.
My short skirt is
initiation, appreciation, excitation.

But mainly my short skirt
and everything under it
is mine, mine, mine.

THINGS THAT GIVE US PLEASURE

When Zena tickles the inside of my arm
all the way to my elbow
Jumping Night Dancer
my legs at his side, the wind,
the rush
Knowing the answer
Warm soapy water
Learning the history of Russia
Speaking Arabic
Rice
Curry
Chicken
Putting on bright red lipstick
Straightening my hair
Curling my hair
Covering my hair
Flan
Halvah

Baklava

Gelato

Macaroons

Pinkberry

Standing on my head

Doing a split

Running faster

Saving minks

Saving whales

Saving plastic bags

Sushi

My mother's happiness

Being in the river

The ocean

The pool with my friends

Sleepovers

Fitting into the new smaller jeans

My mother putting a washcloth

on my forehead when I have a fever

Trying on bras

The way the trees rustle

when birds come back

GIRL FACT

More than 900 million girls and women are
living on less than a dollar a day.

FIVE COWS AND A CALF

THE STORY

I'm not sure the exact day he decided to sell me. There was a drought. For three months it was like someone erased all the green from the bushes and grass and trees. The earth turned brown. The rivers became stone. Everywhere was dust. In our mouths, our beds, our dreams. The cows. It was all about the cows.

I am a Masai girl. I live in Kenya. My name is Mary. I am fifteen. I was fourteen when it all happened. For as long as I can remember we have moved. I like moving. We move with the cows. They eat and then, when they need more grass to eat, we move again. Our people believe the rain god Ngai gave all the cattle to the Masai for safekeeping. We live on milk and blood.

I was in school. I was smart. I could remember things and I learned to write faster than anyone in my class. The teachers said I could go far.

My father was very powerful. He had many children and cows. At least forty children, but they don't count girls so it's hard to tell. He had married off several of my older sisters before me. Sold them to old men and they had each gone far away. Sold them for cows. I knew that before they became wives they were cut with a razor. I knew they were in enormous pain. Their faces changed. And they stopped asking questions. I didn't want to stop asking questions.

WHEN IT CHANGED

The drought got worse. The cows were so skinny their bones were sticking through their skin. They were exhausted and could hardly move. No grass, no water. Some were dying. My father was becoming poor. He got grumpier by the day. I knew the morning they called us into the field. I could tell by their expressions. Ntotya was dead. That was my mother's cow. My mother was crying. I don't remember her crying before. I realized later she was crying for me. The vultures were already there. They are so patient. They can wait forever.

My father did not wait. I heard them talking. An old man was sitting with him. They would pick a date. My father's voice was harsh. It was about my dowry, the number of cows. The old man was missing an eye. I tried to imagine kissing him. I tried to imagine never reading again. I tried to imagine them cutting between my legs.

RUNNING AWAY

I didn't even wash. I had three hundred shillings in my pocket. I saved them instead of buying my Christmas clothes. I escorted my friend Sintoyia down the road. Then I just kept walking. I had heard of a Rescue Center for girls. It was far away. At first I felt freedom in my step, but after six hours it grew dark. I tried to rest under a tree. The wild sounds of hyenas and birds wouldn't let me sleep. It was as if they were screaming at me. I tried to picture the face of a friendly mama greeting me at the house but then I would see my father's angry face. He had his stick, a gun, and he was killing me. My heart beat in wild rhythm with the thirsty cicadas as I stumbled along the dark road. I walked away from my father's house, my family, my life. I walked way out in the wilderness, into night. I walked beyond myself.

I was covered in dust when I arrived. Mama Naanyo was laughing, happy. It was like she had been waiting for me. There were so many other girls who had walked long distances. We were the girls who had to go. We were the girls who left our father's house. We were the girls who changed tradition. We were a tribe and we grew close. We went to school. I learned that even if there was a drought, my father had no right sell me. It was slavery. I learned that my clitoris belonged to me and could bring me pleasure when I got married. I learned that I can be anything and that girls can know as much as boys and we should be counted.

I found out later that after I ran away my father beat my mother but she stood up for me. My three younger sisters fled into the land. My mother went to the elders.

After a year Mama Naanyo called me in. She said *I have talked to your father and he will see you.* She said *I think you are that strong. I think he is ready to accept you.*

THE RECONCILIATION

My whole body was shaking when I came into his house. I didn't know if I could stand up. My father was there next to my mother and his four wives. He seemed so old and so much weaker than I remembered him. I held on to Mama Naanyo. It had been a whole year. I knew I looked good. I had pretty clothes and I had changed. I was a strong confident girl. Everyone started crying. Even my father. Then my sisters came in. They had been living outside all year, in the fields. There was this screaming crying hugging that sisters do. Then I saw my father really looking at me. He could see I was no longer afraid. He could see I had walked through to the other side. He stood and slowly hugged me. He said I had done good and he thanked Mama Naanyo for making me respectable, then he spoke a miracle. He said he would accept me back into his family. He said he would not cut or sell my sisters either.

My mother was so happy. She has always given everything. Pocket money and clothes. This time she risked being beaten.

In spite of what was done to her, she asked the elders for my freedom.

There was a ceremony. All our tribe took the day off from the market to welcome me back. I stood in front and talked. I looked at the women sitting on the ground with their gorgeous beads and colorful cloth, shaved heads and open faces. I looked at my mother, my stepmothers, my sisters, and all my brothers. I loved my family. I loved our wandering and our ways. I loved the way we took care of the land. I loved sharing with the elephants and lions and zebras and cows. I loved that our culture had survived. I loved all of this, but I knew our life could be better.

My father was willing to sell me for five cows and a calf and a couple of blankets. That is about thirty thousand shillings. But when I am educated I will make more money. I will build him a house. I will take care of all of them.

I looked at the women in my family who had been sold, who had been cut when they were my age. My auntie was laughing. The rest of them were singing. This was all our celebration. This was all our beginning. Then in the middle of all of this I noticed we were soaking wet 'cause it was raining.

I AM AN EMOTIONAL CREATURE

I love being a girl.
I can feel what you're feeling
as you're feeling it inside
the feeling
before.
I am an emotional creature.
Things do not come to me
as intellectual theories or hard-shaped ideas.
They pulse through my organs and legs
and burn up my ears.
I know when your girlfriend's really pissed off
even though she appears to give you what
    you want.
I know when a storm is coming.
I can feel the invisible stirrings in the air.
I can tell you he won't call back.
It's a vibe I share.

I am an emotional creature.
I love that I do not take things lightly.
Everything is intense to me.
The way I walk in the street.
The way my mother wakes me up.
The way I hear bad news.
The way it's unbearable when I lose.

I am an emotional creature.
I am connected to everything and everyone.
I was born like that.
Don't you dare say all negative that it's a
     teenage thing
or it's only only because I'm a girl.
These feelings make me better.
They make me ready.
They make me present.
They make me strong.

I am an emotional creature.
There is a particular way of knowing.
It's like the older women somehow forgot.
I rejoice that it's still in my body.

I know when the coconut's about to fall.
I know that we've pushed the earth too far.
I know my father isn't coming back.
That no one's prepared for the fire.

I know that lipstick means
more than show.
I know that boys feel super-insecure
and so-called terrorists are made, not born.
I know that one kiss can take
away all my decision-making ability
and sometimes, you know, it should.

This is not extreme.
It's a girl thing.
What we would all be
if the big door inside us flew open.
Don't tell me not to cry
To calm it down
Not to be so extreme
To be reasonable.
I am an emotional creature.
It's how the earth got made.
How the wind continues to pollinate.
You don't tell the Atlantic Ocean
to behave.

I am an emotional creature.
Why would you want to shut me down
or turn me off?
I am your remaining memory.
I am connecting you to your source.
Nothing's been diluted.

Nothing's leaked out.
I can take you back.

I love that I can feel the inside
of the feelings in you,
even if it stops my life
even if it hurts too much
or takes me off track
even if it breaks my heart.
It makes me responsible.
I am an emotional
I am an emotional, devotional,
incandotional creature.
And I love, hear me,
love love love
being a girl.

I DANCE (III)

I dance to be here
I dance to disappear
I dance 'cause I can and I will

I dance with the gypsies
And with those in the churches
I dance with the witches and fairies
and freaks
I dance into the green reaches of earth
I dance with the ones who get left by
    the road
I dance until all of us are sweaty and one
I dance on tables
On rooftops
In stairways
I dance when I want to scream
and claw and scratch and punch

I dance till I am wild, till I'm crazy
I dance till I'm brave and undone
I dance frenzy
I dance danger
I dance girl
I dance 'cause I cannot stop
I dance 'cause I feel that much
I dance 'cause I love you
I love you, I love you
Now, don't just stand there
with your arms all crossed
My skin is a map
My belly's on fire
Come with me
Dance with me
All of you
Higher
Higher

EPILOGUE:
MANIFESTA TO YOUNG WOMEN AND GIRLS

HERE'S WHAT YOU WILL BE TOLD:

Find a man

Seek protection

The world is scary

Don't go out

You are weak

Don't care so much

They're only animals

Don't be so intense

Don't cry so much

You can't trust anyone

Don't talk to strangers

People will take advantage of you

Close your legs

Girls aren't good with:

Numbers

Facts

Making difficult decisions

Lifting things

Putting things together

International news

Flying planes

Being in charge.

If he rapes you, surrender,

you will get killed trying to defend yourself

Don't travel alone

You are nothing without a man

Don't make the first move,

wait for him to notice you

Don't be too loud

Follow the crowd

Obey the laws

Don't know too much

Tone it down

Find someone rich

It's how you look that matters,

not what you think.

HERE'S WHAT I'M TELLING YOU:

Everyone's making everything up

There is no one in charge except for those

who pretend to be

No one is coming

No one is going to

Rescue you
Mind-read your needs
Know your body better than you

Always fight back
Ask for it
Say you want it
Cherish your solitude
Take trains by yourself to places
you have never been
Sleep out alone under the stars
Learn how to drive a stick shift
Go so far away that you stop being afraid of
not coming back
Say no when you don't want to do something
Say yes if your instincts are strong
even if everyone around you disagrees
Decide whether you want to be liked or admired
Decide if fitting in is more important than finding out
what you're doing here
Believe in kissing
Fight for tenderness
Care as much as you do
Cry as much as you want
Insist the world be theater
and love the drama
Take your time
Move as fast as you do
as long as it's your speed.

Ask yourself these questions:

Why am I whispering when I have something to say?

Why am I adding a question mark at the end

of all my sentences?

Why am I apologizing every time I express my needs?

Why am I hunching over?

Starving myself when I love food?

Pretending it doesn't mean that much to me?

Hurting myself when I mean to scream?

Why am I waiting

Whining

Pining

Fitting in?

You know the truth:

Sometimes it does hurt that much

Horses can feel love

Your mother wanted more than that

It's easier to be mean than smart

But that isn't who you are.

ACKNOWLEDGMENTS

I want to thank the following people who have either read, edited, or nurtured *Emotional Creature* into being: Allison Prouty, Amy Squires, Beth Dozoretz, Brian McLendon, Cari Ross, Carol Gilligan, Cecile Lipworth, Christine Schuler Deschryver, Diana DeVegh, Donna Karan, Emily Scott Pottruck, Elizabeth Lesser, George Lane, Golzar Selbe, Ilene Chaiken, James Lecesne, Jane Fonda, Kate Fisher, Judy Corcoran, Kate Medina, Katherine McFate, Kerry Washington, Kim Guzowski, Laura Waleryszak, Linda Pope, Marie Cecile Renauld, Mark Matousek, Mellody Hobson, Meredith Kaffel, Molly Kawachi, Nancy Rose, Naomi Klein, Nicoletta Billi, Nikki Noto, Pat Mitchell, Paula Allen, Purva Panday, Rada Boric, Rosario Dawson, Salma Hayek, Shael Norris, Sheryl Sandberg, Susan Swan.

I thank Frankie Jones for her guidance and faith in this book and Jill Schwartzman for jumping in with such energy and care.

I thank Charlotte Sheedy for being in my corner for over thirty years, for her fierceness and love.

I thank Kim Rosen for long nights and listening again and again, and Tony Montenieri for his constancy and profound attention.

I thank my son, Dylan, for freeing my heart, and my mother, Chris, for bringing me here.

I would like to thank the brave and brilliant girls around the world who inspired this book.

I would also like to thank a group of brilliant women who so generously gave of themselves to shape the curriculum that will one day accompany this book.

V-GIRLS ADVISORY CIRCLE

Lyn Mikel Brown

Marie Celestin

Carol Gilligan

Lynda Kennedy

Kelly Kinnish

Michele Ozumba

Cydney Pullman

Jule Jo Ramirez

Lillian Rivera

Sil Reynolds

Deborah Tolman

Niobe Way

Emily Wylie

ADDITIONAL CONTRIBUTORS TO THE CURRICULUM

Yalitiza Garcia

Nicole Butterfield

Maureen Ferris

Lisa Beth Miller

Jennifer Gandin Le

Christopher Gandin Le

GIRL FACT SOURCES

ix   **Your left lung:** U.S. Department of Health & Human Services, National Insitutes of Health, National Heart, Lung and Blood Institute, "Diseases and Conditions Index: Lung Diseases: How the Lungs Work" (www.nhlbi.nih.gov/health/dci/Diseases/hlw/hlw_all.html).

17   **One in five U.S. high school girls:** Girls Inc. press release, "The Supergirl Dilemma: Girls Grapple with the Mounting Pressure of Expectations," October 12, 2006.

22   **Despite years of evaluation:** Douglas Kirby, *Emerging Answers: Research Findings on Programs to Reduce Teen Pregnancy* (Washington, D.C.: National Campaign to Prevent Teen Pregnancy, 2001); Peter S. Bearman and Hannah Brückner, "Promising the Future: Virginity Pledges and First Intercourse," *American Journal of Sociology*, 106(4) (2001): 859–912; Hannah Brückner and Peter Bearman, "After the Promise: the STD Consequences of Adolescent Virginity Pledges," *Journal of Adolescent Health*, 36(4) (2005): 271–278.

22   **Six in ten American teens:** Ellen Goodman, "The Truth About Teens and Sex." *The Boston Globe*, January 3, 2009.

28   **In Africa, about three million girls a year:** Nahid Toubia, *Caring for Women with Circumcision: A Technical Manual for Health Care Providers*

(New York: Research, Action and Information Network for the Bodily Integrity of Women [RAINBO], 1999).

37 **Research has shown:** Sumru Erkut and Allison J. Tracy, *Sports as Protective of Girls' High-Risk Sexual Behavior* (Wellesley, Mass.: Wellesley Centers for Women, 2005).

60 **When a group of children who were interviewed:** Sandra Solovay, *Tipping the Scales of Justice: Fighting Weight-Based Discrimination* (Amherst, N.Y.: Prometheus Books, 2000).

60 **The mortality rate associated with anorexia nervosa:** South Carolina Department of Mental Health, "Eating Disorder Statistics" (www.state.sc.us/dmh/anorexia/statistics.htm).

70 **About one in three:** Alabama Coalition Against Domestic Violence (www.acadv.org/dating.html).

74 **Girls between thirteen and eighteen:** Unicef, "Gender Equality: The Situation of Women and Girls: Facts and Figures" (www.unicef.org/gender/index_factsandfigures.html).

81 **Barbie was based:** Russ Kick, *50 Things You're Not Supposed to Know, Volume 2* (New York: The Disinformation Company, 2004).

96 **A new report says:** Save the Children, Especially Vulnerable Children: Child Soldiers (www.voanews.com/english/archive/2005-04/2005-04-25-voa27.cfm).

113 **An estimated one hundred million girls:** International Labour Organization, International Programme on the Elimination of Child Labour, "World Day 2009: Give Girls a Chance: End Child Labour" (www.ilo.org/ipec/Campaignandadvocacy/WDACL/WorldDay2009/lang--en/index.htm).

128 **More than 900 million girls and women:** Plan's "Because I Am a Girl" campaign, "The Facts" (www.plan-uk.org/becauseiamagirl/thefacts).

DISCUSSION QUESTIONS

If you've been inspired by reading *I Am an Emotional Creature*, consider talking about the book with your friends or even starting a discussion group. The guide below is intended to help readers explore the book, and reflect and discuss the text as it pertains to themselves and their community. Want to learn more about discussion groups or connecting with others who loved the book? Check out www.v-girls.org.

YOU TELL ME HOW TO BE A GIRL IN 2010
- What is it like to be a girl today?
- What makes you angry? What inspires you?
- How can you create change in the world?
- Do you see a division between the "haves" and the "have nots" in the world? How does that make you feel? Do you see a solution?
- Learn more about references in the monologue that you are

unfamiliar with and share what you have learned with your group.

LET ME IN
- Have you ever wanted to fit in, or felt excluded? Have you ever excluded others?
- Why do we want to fit in or exclude others?
- Why are we afraid to be different?
- What would the world be like without bullies, cliques, or peer pressure?
- What are some of the consequences of excluding others? Can you think of any examples in your school or community?

WHAT DON'T YOU LIKE ABOUT BEING A GIRL?
- Respond to the questions posed in the monologues. What don't you like about being a girl?
- Can girls "do things better"?
- Can there be good things about being a "bad girl"? Can there be bad things about being a "good girl"? How can you focus more on what you like about yourself?

BAD BOYS
- How is the character trying to deal with her emotions?
- Do your parents have unrealistic expectations for who they want you to be?
- Whom do you feel that you can turn to when you have a problem?

- Why do you think the character chooses a boyfriend who is a "bad boy"?
- Have you ever been tempted by a "bad boy"? How did you respond?

WHAT I WISH I COULD SAY TO MY MOTHER
- Do you feel misunderstood by your parents, family members, or caretakers? How?
- What questions would you like to ask your mother?
- What would you like for your mother to know about you?
- Why do you think relationships between mothers and daughters are challenging?

IT'S NOT A BABY, IT'S A MAYBE
- How does facing the unknown bring up mixed emotions? How does facing the unknown conjure up our greatest fears?
- If you were in this character's situation, where would you turn for help?
- What does the character mean when she says she was practicing abstinence but didn't know how to apply it?
- Do you think young people are properly educated about sex and unplanned pregnancy?

WHAT'S A GOOD GIRL?
- How would you define a "good girl"?
- Would you define yourself as one? Explain.

DON'T

- Have you ever been told you could not do something or been treated differently because you are a girl?
- How can education create opportunity for girls?

WOULD YOU RATHER

- Do you ever have to make choices when you don't like any of the options you have to choose from? What do you do in those situations?
- Do you ever feel pressure from your friends to make choices you aren't comfortable with?
- How can you find peace within yourself when there seem to be more questions than answers?

STEPHANIED

- Have you ever had a crush? A girl crush?
- Does a girl crush have to be sexual?
- What do you think about the character not identifying as gay or straight? What do you think society thinks?

MOVING TOWARD THE HOOP

- What identities have you been "ducking or too defiantly embracing"?
- How can sports empower girls?
- Have you played sports? Have they impacted you?
- What stereotypes are there about female athletes?
- What would it mean to lose your identity? To change it?

SOPHIE ET APOLLINE, OR, WHY FRENCH GIRLS SMOKE

- What are the qualities of a good friend?
- How are your friendships important to you?
- Do you think girls your age are in a rush to grow up? Do you ever feel conflicted about growing up?
- In this monologue, the girls smoke sometimes when they feel stressed out. How do you deal with stress?

THINGS I HEARD ABOUT SEX

- Where do you think young people get most of their information about sex?
- Whom can you go to with your questions about sex?
- Why do you think it is important for girls to be informed about sex?

I DANCE

- How does dancing make you feel?
- Do you dance? Why or why not? If you do, whom do you dance for?
- What are the different ways you express yourself when you are happy, sad, or mad?
- How can you learn about yourself and others through dance?

I BUILD IT WITH STONE

- What does "sacred" mean?
- What is sacred to you? What are you devoted to?
- How do you express devotion?

- Does devotion have to be religious? Why or why not?
- Why do you think people have devotional practices?

HUNGER BLOG

- What does "beautiful is a country with gates around it" mean? Do you ever feel that way?
- What do you like to eat? Do you ever feel anxious about eating?
- What advice would you give to a girl struggling with an eating disorder?
- Why do you think so many girls don't like what they see in the mirror?

THE JOKE ABOUT MY NOSE

- What part of your body do you think people notice the most?
- Do you think "funny people enjoy everything"?
- Why do you think the character needs or wants to make a joke about her nose?
- What do you think about young women having plastic surgery?
- Do you feel pressured to look different than you do now? Where does this pressure come from?

DEAR RIHANNA

- What does a healthy relationship look like to you?
- Why do you think it is difficult for people who are abused by their partners to leave or end the relationship?
- Do you think it is possible for a person who has abused his or her partner to change?

- Have you ever wanted to "push boy delete"? Is this possible or beneficial?
- What role do celebrities have in your life? How are you affected by them?
- How do we both envy and destroy celebrities?

I HAVE 35 MINUTES BEFORE HE COMES LOOKING FOR ME

- What is the role of power and fear in this monologue?
- How can power and fear lead to violence?
- How does the character in this monologue show bravery?
- How do you think you would respond if you were in her situation?

FREE BARBIE

- Have you ever played with a Barbie? Has she influenced your life?
- What message does Chang Ying want to share?
- What do you think about Chang Ying's comparison between Barbie's dream house and her "nightmare house"?
- What do you think "free" Barbie would say or do? Would she look different?
- Does this monologue make you think differently about Barbie?

SKY SKY SKY

- How are the characters in the monologue similar and different? How are they connected?
- How do the characters challenge what is expected of them?

- What consequences might there be for standing up for what you believe in? Would this change your actions?
- What do you already know about the conflict between Israel and Palestine? What do you want to know more about?

THE WALL
- When have you felt "walled in" or "walled out" in your own life? What, or who, caused you to feel this way? How did you cope with this feeling?
- What does it feel like to take a stand for something you believe in, even when it is not the popular choice?
- What do you imagine it might feel like to be a young person living in a conflict zone?

A TEENAGE GIRL'S GUIDE TO SURVIVING SEX SLAVERY
- How do you think the rules the character shares apply "to any girl anywhere in the world"?
- Where does the character find hope within her desperate situation? Does she ever lose hope?
- What does the character mean when she says, "No one can take anything from you if you do not give it to them"?
- How is the character a survivor? How are you a survivor?

REFUSER
- What does it mean to be a "refuser"?
- Who are the refusers who inspire you?
- Learn more about the refusers included in the monologue. Which individuals or issues speak to you?

- How can you be a refuser in your everyday life?
- Do you think young people can make an impact as refusers?

WHAT DO YOU LIKE ABOUT BEING A GIRL?
- What's your favorite thing about being a girl?
- What are some misconceptions about girls?

ASKING THE QUESTION
- Why is it so hard to "ask the question" to use contraception with a sexual partner?
- Do you think guys don't want to wear condoms? Why wouldn't they?
- What advice would you give a friend who needs to "ask the question"?
- Do you ever "make people up" and imagine what others are thinking or feeling, as the character in the monologue does?
- What role does honesty play in a healthy romantic or sexual relationship?

THINGS I LIKE ABOUT MY BODY
- What do you like about your body?
- What makes you feel strong and confident?
- What outside influences affect how girls feel about their bodies?
- What would the world be like if we loved and appreciated one another as we are?

MY SHORT SKIRT

- How can you challenge the belief that girls "ask for it" if they dress in a certain way?
- How do women look in real life versus in the media? How does this influence you?
- What do you find beautiful in real life?
- How can your clothing express defiance or empowerment?

THINGS THAT GIVE US PLEASURE

- What gives you pleasure?
- Do you ever feel like you are doing things just to make other people happy?
- How can you focus on what gives you pleasure, rather than seeking to please others?

FIVE COWS AND A CALF

- Why do you think gender violence is so common throughout the world and throughout history?
- What does your culture expect from you as a girl?
- How can you challenge these expectations?
- Where would you like to have reconciliation for yourself, in your family, in your friendships, or in other aspects of your life?
- What is FGM? What do you think about the practice? Do you think it is possible for cultural attitudes about FGM to change? How?
- Do you know of any places where long-practiced traditions have changed?

I AM AN EMOTIONAL CREATURE
- What is an emotional creature?
- How are you an emotional creature?
- What have you been told to shut down or turn off?
- Have you ever been told you are too much of something? Too intense, wild, caring, angry, idealistic, etc.? How do you challenge these assumptions?
- What would happen if you let the big door inside you fly open? What would happen if we all did?

EPILOGUE: MANIFESTA TO YOUNG WOMEN AND GIRLS
- How can you keep your heart open?
- What are your hopes and dreams? Who do you want to be, where do you want to go, and what do you want to learn?
- How can you be true to yourself when there are so many things that other people want you to do and be?
- How do you want to be an activist in the world?
- What issues and causes are important to you?

ABOUT THE AUTHOR

EVE ENSLER is an internationally bestselling author and an acclaimed playwright whose works for the stage include *The Vagina Monologues, Necessary Targets,* and *The Good Body.* She is the author of *Insecure at Last,* a political memoir. Ensler is the founder of V-Day (vday.org), the global movement to end violence against women and girls. In the last decade, V-Day has raised more than $70 million for grassroots groups that work to end violence against women and girls around the world. Eve Ensler lives in Paris and New York City.